RHINOCEROS
AND OTHER PLAYS

RHINOCEROS
AND OTHER PLAYS

BY EUGÈNE IONESCO

▲

Translated by Derek Prouse

GROVE PRESS, INC.

NEW YORK

CONTENTS

Other works by
Eugène Ionesco

THE LESSON
THE CHAIRS
THE BALD SOPRANO
JACK *Or* THE SUBMISSION

AMÉDÉÉ *Or* HOW TO GET RID OF IT
THE NEW TENANT
VICTIMS OF DUTY

THE KILLER
IMPROVISATION
MAID TO MARRY

RHINOCEROS

Main Cast List for the first Paris Production

BERENGER	Jean-Louis Barrault
JEAN	William Sabatier
DAISY	Simone Valère
DUDARD	Gabriel Cattand
THE LOGICIAN	Jean Parédès
THE WAITRESS	Jane Martel
THE HOUSEWIFE	Marie-Hélène Dasté
THE OLD GENTLEMAN	Robert Lombard
MRS. BOEUF	Simone Paris
MR. PAPILLON	Michel Bertay

Main Cast List for the first London Production

BERENGER	Laurence Olivier
JEAN	Duncan Macrae
DAISY	Joan Plowright
DUDARD	Alan Webb
THE LOGICIAN	Geoffrey Dunn
THE WAITRESS	Monica Evans
THE HOUSEWIFE	Hazel Hughes
THE OLD GENTLEMAN	Michael Bates
MRS. BOEUF	Gladys Henson
MR. PAPILLON	Miles Malleson

RHINOCEROS

A Play in Three Acts and Four Scenes.

First produced in Paris by Jean-Louis Barrault at the Odéon, the
25th January, 1960.

First produced in London by Orson Welles at the Royal Court Theatre,
the 28th April, 1960.

CHARACTERS

	Scene			
JEAN	1st		3rd	
BERENGER	1st	2nd	3rd	4th
THE WAITRESS	1st			
THE GROCER	1st			
THE GROCER'S WIFE	1st			
THE OLD GENTLEMAN	1st			
THE LOGICIAN	1st			
THE HOUSEWIFE	1st			
THE CAFÉ PROPRIETOR	1st			
DAISY	1st	2nd		4th
MR. PAPILLON		2nd		
DUDARD		2nd		4th
BOTARD		2nd		
MRS. BOEUF		2nd		
A FIREMAN		2nd		
THE LITTLE OLD MAN			3rd	
THE LITTLE OLD MAN'S WIFE			3rd	
And a lot of Rhinoceros heads				

ACT ONE

The scene is a square in a small provincial town. Up-stage a house
composed of a ground floor and one storey. The ground floor is the
window of a grocer's shop. The entrance is up two or three steps through

a glass-paned door. The word EPICERIE is written in bold letters above the shop window. The two windows on the first floor are the living quarters of the grocer and his wife. The shop is up-stage, but slightly to the left, not far from the wings. In the distance a church steeple is visible above the grocer's house. Between the shop and the left of the stage there is a little street in perspective. To the right, slightly at an angle, is the front of a café. Above the café, one floor with a window; in front, the café terrace; several chairs and tables reach almost to centre stage. A dusty tree stands near the terrace chairs. Blue sky; harsh light; very white walls. The time is almost mid-day on a Sunday in summer-time. JEAN *and* BERENGER *will sit at one of the terrace tables.*

   [*The sound of church bells is heard, which stop a few moments before the curtain rises. When the curtain rises, a woman carrying a basket of provisions under one arm and a cat under the other crosses the stage in silence from right to left. As she does so, the* GROCER'S WIFE *opens her shop door and watches her pass.*]

GROCER'S WIFE: Oh that woman gets on my nerves! [*To her husband who is in the shop:*] Too stuck-up to buy from us nowadays. [*The* GROCER'S WIFE *leaves; the stage is empty for a few moments.*]

   [JEAN *enters right, at the same time as* BERENGER *enters left.* JEAN *is very fastidiously dressed: brown suit, red tie, stiff collar, brown hat. He has a reddish face. His shoes are yellow and well-polished.* BERENGER *is unshaven and hatless, with unkempt hair and creased clothes; everything about him indicates negligence. He seems weary, half-asleep; from time to time he yawns.*]

JEAN: [*advancing from right*] Oh, so you managed to get here at last, Berenger!

BERENGER: [*advancing from left*] Morning, Jean!

JEAN: Late as usual, of course. [*He looks at his wrist watch.*] Our appointment was for 11.30. And now it's practically mid-day.

BERENGER: I'm sorry. Have you been waiting long?

JEAN: No, I've only just arrived myself, as you saw.

   [*They go and sit at one of the tables on the café terrace.*]

BERENGER: In that case I don't feel so bad, if you've only just . . .

JEAN: It's different with me. I don't like waiting; I've no time to waste. And as you're never on time, I come late on purpose— at a time when I presume you'll be there.

BERENGER: You're right . . . quite right, but . . .

JEAN: Now don't try to pretend you're ever on time!

BERENGER: No, of course not . . . I wouldn't say that.

[JEAN *and* BERENGER *have sat down.*]

JEAN: There you are, you see!

BERENGER: What are you drinking?

JEAN: You mean to say you've got a thirst even at this time in the morning?

BERENGER: It's so hot and dry.

JEAN: The more you drink the thirstier you get, popular science tells us that . . .

BERENGER: It would be less dry, and we'd be less thirsty, if they'd invent us some scientific clouds in the sky.

JEAN: [*studying* BERENGER *closely*] That wouldn't help you any. You're not thirsty for water, Berenger . . .

BERENGER: I don't understand what you mean.

JEAN: You know perfectly well what I mean. I'm talking about your parched throat. That's a territory that can't get enough!

BERENGER: To compare my throat to a piece of land seems . . .

JEAN: [*interrupting him*] You're in a bad way, my friend.

BERENGER: In a bad way? You think so?

JEAN: I'm not blind, you know. You're dropping with fatigue. You've gone without your sleep again, you yawn all the time, you're dead-tired . . .

BERENGER: There is something the matter with my hair . . .

JEAN: You reek of alcohol.

BERENGER: I have got a bit of a hang-over, it's true!

JEAN: It's the same every Sunday morning—not to mention the other days of the week.

BERENGER: Oh no, it's less frequent during the week, because of the office . . .

JEAN: And what's happened to your tie? Lost it during your orgy, I suppose!

BERENGER: [*putting his hand to his neck*] You're right. That's funny! Whatever could I have done with it?

JEAN: [*taking a tie out of his coat pocket*] Here, put this one on.

BERENGER: Oh thank you, that is kind. [*He puts on the tie.*]

JEAN: [*while* BERENGER *is unskilfully tying his tie*] Your hair's all over the place.

[BERENGER *runs his fingers through his hair.*]

Here, here's a comb! [*He takes a comb from his other pocket.*]

BERENGER: [*taking the comb*] Thank you. [*He vaguely combs his hair.*]

JEAN: You haven't even shaved! Just take a look at yourself!

[*He takes a mirror from his inside pocket, hands it to* BERENGER, *who looks at himself; as he does so, he examines his tongue.*]

BERENGER: My tongue's all coated.

JEAN: [*taking the mirror and putting it back in his pocket*] I'm not surprised! [*He takes back the comb as well, which* BERENGER *offers to him, and puts it in his pocket.*] You're heading for cirrhosis, my friend.

BERENGER: [*worried*] Do you think so?

JEAN: [*to* BERENGER, *who wants to give him back his tie*] Keep the tie, I've got plenty more.

BERENGER: [*admiringly*] You always look so immaculate.

JEAN: [*continuing his inspection of* BERENGER] Your clothes are all crumpled, they're a disgrace! Your shirt is downright filthy, and your shoes . . . [BERENGER *tries to hide his feet under the table.*] Your shoes haven't been touched. What a mess you're in! And look at your shoulders . . .

BERENGER: What's the matter with my shoulders?

JEAN: Turn round! Come on, turn round! You've been leaning against some wall. [BERENGER *holds his hand out docilely to* JEAN.] No, I haven't got a brush with me; it would make my pockets bulge. [*Still docile,* BERENGER *flicks his shoulders to get rid of the white dust;* JEAN *averts his head.*] Heavens! Where did you get all that from?

BERENGER: I don't remember.

JEAN: It's a positive disgrace! I feel ashamed to be your friend.

BERENGER: You're very hard on me . . .

JEAN: I've every reason to be.

BERENGER: Listen, Jean. There are so few distractions in this town—I get so bored. I'm not made for the work I'm doing . . . every day at the office, eight hours a day—and only three weeks' holiday a year! When Saturday night comes round I feel exhausted and so—you know how it is—just to relax . . .

JEAN: My dear man, everybody has to work. I spend eight hours a day in the office the same as everyone else. And I only get three weeks off a year, but even so you don't catch me . . . Will-power, my good man!

BERENGER: But everybody hasn't got as much will-power as you have. I can't get used to it. I just can't get used to life.

JEAN: Everybody has to get used to it. Or do you consider yourself some superior being?

BERENGER: I don't pretend to be . . .

JEAN: [interrupting him] I'm just as good as you are; I think with all due modesty I may say I'm better. The superior man is the man who fulfils his duty.

BERENGER: What duty?

JEAN: His duty . . . His duty as an employee, for example.

BERENGER: Oh yes, his duty as an employee . . .

JEAN: Where did your debauch take place last night? If you can remember!

BERENGER: We were celebrating Auguste's birthday, our friend Auguste . . .

JEAN: Our friend Auguste? Nobody invited me to our friend Auguste's birthday . . .

[At this moment a noise is heard, far off, but swiftly approaching, of a beast panting in its headlong course, and of a long trumpeting.]

BERENGER: I couldn't refuse. It wouldn't have been nice . . .

JEAN: Did I go there?

BERENGER: Well, perhaps it was because you weren't invited.

WAITRESS: [coming out of café] Good morning, gentlemen. Can I get you something to drink?

[The noise becomes very loud.]

JEAN: [*to* BERENGER, *almost shouting to make himself heard above the noise which he has not become conscious of*] True, I was not invited. That honour was denied me. But in any case, I can assure you, that even if I had been invited, I would not have gone, because . . .

[*The noise has become intense.*]

What's going on?

[*The noise of a powerful, heavy animal, galloping at great speed is heard very close; the sound of panting.*]

Whatever is it?

WAITRESS: Whatever is it?

[BERENGER, *still listless without appearing to hear anything at all, replies tranquilly to* JEAN *about the invitation; his lips move but one doesn't hear what he says;* JEAN *bounds to his feet, knocking his chair over as he does so, looks off left pointing, whilst* BERENGER, *still a little dopey, remains seated.*]

JEAN: Oh, a rhinoceros!

[*The noise made by the animal dies away swiftly and one can already hear the following words. The whole of this scene must be played very fast, each repeating in swift succession: 'Oh, a rhinoceros!'*]

WAITRESS: Oh, a rhinoceros!

GROCER'S WIFE: [*sticks her head out of her shop doorway*] Oh, a rhinoceros! [*To her husband still inside the shop:*] Quick, come and look; it's a rhinoceros!

[*They are all looking off left after the animal.*]

JEAN: It's rushing straight ahead, brushing up against the shop windows.

GROCER: [*in his shop*] Whereabouts?

WAITRESS: [*putting her hands on her hips*] Well!

GROCER'S WIFE: [*to her husband who is still in shop*] Come and look!

[*At this moment the* GROCER *puts his head out.*]

GROCER: Oh, a rhinoceros!

LOGICIAN: [*entering quickly left*] A rhinoceros going full-tilt on the opposite pavement!

[*All these speeches from the time when* JEAN *says* 'Oh, a rhinoceros' *are practically simultaneous. A woman is heard crying 'Ah!' She appears. She runs to the centre-stage; it is a HOUSEWIFE with a basket on her arm; once arrived centre-stage she drops her basket; the contents scatter all over the stage, a bottle breaks, but she does not drop her cat.]*

HOUSEWIFE: Ah! Oh!

[An elegant OLD GENTLEMAN comes from left stage, after the HOUSEWIFE, rushes into the GROCER's shop, knocks into the GROCER and his WIFE, whilst the LOGICIAN installs himself against the back wall on the left of the grocery entrance. JEAN and the WAITRESS, standing, and BERENGER, still apathetically seated, together form another group. At the same time, coming from the left, cries of 'Oh' and 'Ah' and the noise of people running have been heard. The dust raised by the animal spreads over the stage.]

CAFÉ PROPRIETOR: *[sticking his head out of the first-floor window]* What's going on?

OLD GENTLEMAN: *[disappearing behind the GROCER and his WIFE]* Excuse me, please!

[The OLD GENTLEMAN is elegantly dressed, with white spats, a soft hat and an ivory-handled cane; the LOGICIAN, propped up against the wall has a little grey moustache, an eyeglass, and is wearing a straw hat.]

GROCER'S WIFE: *[jostled and jostling her husband; to the OLD GENTLEMAN]* Watch out with that stick!

GROCER: Look where you're going, can't you!

[The head of the OLD GENTLEMAN is seen behind the GROCER and his WIFE.]

WAITRESS: *[to the PROPRIETOR]* A rhinoceros!

PROPRIETOR: *[to the WAITRESS from his window]* You're seeing things. *[He sees the rhinoceros:]* Well, I'll be . . . !

HOUSEWIFE: Ah!

[The 'Ohs' and 'Ahs' from off-stage form a background accompaniment to her 'Ah'. She has dropped her basket, her provisions and the bottle, but has nevertheless kept tight hold of her cat which she carries under her other arm.]

There, they frightened the poor pussy!

PROPRIETOR: [*still looking off left, following the distant course of the animal as the noises fade; hooves, trumpetings, etc.*]

[BERENGER *sleepily averts his head a little on account of the dust, but says nothing; he simply makes a grimace.*]

Well, of all things!

JEAN: [*also averting his head a little, but very much awake*] Well, of all things! [*He sneezes.*]

HOUSEWIFE: [*she is centre-stage but turned towards left; her provisions scattered on the ground round her*] Well of all things! [*She sneezes.*]

[*The* OLD GENTLEMAN, GROCER'S WIFE *and* GROCER *up-stage re-opening the glass door of the* GROCER's *shop that the* OLD GENTLEMAN *has closed behind him.*]

ALL THREE: Well, of all things!

JEAN: Well, of all things! [*To* BERENGER:] Did you see that?

[*The noise of the rhinoceros and its trumpeting are now far away; the people are still staring after the animal, all except for* BERENGER *who is still apathetically seated.*]

ALL: [*except* BERENGER] Well, of all things!

BERENGER: [*to* JEAN] It certainly looked as if it was a rhinoceros. It made plenty of dust. [*He takes out a handkerchief and blows his nose.*]

HOUSEWIFE: Well, of all things! Gave me such a scare.

GROCER: [*to the* HOUSEWIFE] Your basket... and all your things...

OLD GENTLEMAN: [*approaching the lady and bending to pick up her things scattered about the stage. He greets her gallantly, raising his hat.*]

PROPRIETOR: Really, these days, you never know...

WAITRESS: Fancy that!

OLD GENTLEMAN: [*to the* HOUSEWIFE] May I help you pick up your things?

HOUSEWIFE: [*to the* OLD GENTLEMAN] Thank you, how very kind! Do put on your hat. Oh, it gave me such a scare!

LOGICIAN: Fear is an irrational thing. It must yield to reason.

WAITRESS: It's already out of sight.

OLD GENTLEMAN: [*to the* HOUSEWIFE *and indicating the* LOGICIAN]
My friend is a logician.

JEAN: [*to* BERENGER] Well, what did you think of that?

WAITRESS: Those animals can certainly travel!

HOUSEWIFE: [*to the* LOGICIAN] Very happy to meet you!

GROCER'S WIFE: [*to the* GROCER] That'll teach her to buy her
things from somebody else!

JEAN: [*to the* PROPRIETOR *and the* WAITRESS] What did you think
of that?

HOUSEWIFE: I still didn't let my cat go.

PROPRIETOR: [*shrugging his shoulders, at window*] You don't often
see that!

HOUSEWIFE: [*to the* LOGICIAN *and the* OLD GENTLEMAN *who is
picking up her provisions*] Would you hold him a moment!

WAITRESS: [*to* JEAN] First time I've seen that!

LOGICIAN: [*to the* HOUSEWIFE, *taking the cat in his arms*] It's not
spiteful, is it?

PROPRIETOR: [*to* JEAN] Went past like a comet!

HOUSEWIFE: [*to the* LOGICIAN] He wouldn't hurt a fly. [*To the
others:*] What happened to my wine?

GROCER: [*to the* HOUSEWIFE] I've got plenty more.

JEAN: [*to* BERENGER] Well, what did you think of that?

GROCER: [*to the* HOUSEWIFE] And good stuff, too!

PROPRIETOR: [*to the* WAITRESS] Don't hang about! Look after
these gentlemen! [*He indicates* BERENGER *and* JEAN. *He withdraws.*]

BERENGER: [*to* JEAN] What did I think of what?

GROCER'S WIFE: [*to the* GROCER] Go and get her another bottle!

JEAN: [*to* BERENGER] Of the rhinoceros, of course! What did you
think I meant?

GROCER: [*to the* HOUSEWIFE] I've got some first-class wine, in
unbreakable bottles! [*He disappears into his shop.*]

LOGICIAN: [*stroking the cat in his arms*] Puss, puss, puss.

WAITRESS: [*to* BERENGER *and* JEAN] What are you drinking?

BERENGER: Two pastis.

WAITRESS: Two pastis—right! [*She walks to the café entrance.*]

HOUSEWIFE: [*picking up her things with the help of the* OLD GENTLE-
MAN] Very kind of you, I'm sure.

WAITRESS: Two pastis! [*She goes into café.*]

OLD GENTLEMAN: [*to the* HOUSEWIFE] Oh, please don't mention
it, it's a pleasure.
    [*The* GROCER'S WIFE *goes into shop.*]

LOGICIAN: [*to the* OLD GENTLEMAN *and the* HOUSEWIFE *picking up
the provisions*] Replace them in an orderly fashion.

JEAN: [*to* BERENGER] Well, what did you think about it?

BERENGER: [*to* JEAN, *not knowing what to say*] Well . . . nothing
. . . it made a lot of dust . . .

GROCER: [*coming out of shop with a bottle of wine; to the* HOUSE-
WIFE] I've some good leeks as well.

LOGICIAN: [*still stroking the cat*] Puss, puss, puss.

GROCER: [*to the* HOUSEWIFE] It's a hundred francs a litre.

HOUSEWIFE: [*paying the* GROCER, *then to the* OLD GENTLEMAN *who
has managed to put everything back in the basket*] Oh, you are
kind! Such a pleasure to come across the old French courtesy.
Not like the young people today!

GROCER: [*taking money*] You should buy from me. You wouldn't
even have to cross the street, and you wouldn't run the risk of
these accidents. [*He goes back into his shop.*]

JEAN: [*who has sat down and is still thinking of the rhinoceros*] But
you must admit it's extraordinary.

OLD GENTLEMAN: [*taking off his hat, and kissing the* HOUSEWIFE'S
hand] It was a great pleasure to meet you!

HOUSEWIFE: [*to the* LOGICIAN] Thank you very much for holding
my cat.
    [*The* LOGICIAN *gives the* HOUSEWIFE *back her cat. The*
    WAITRESS *comes back with drinks.*]

WAITRESS: Two pastis!

JEAN: [*to* BERENGER] You're incorrigible!

OLD GENTLEMAN: [*to the* HOUSEWIFE] May I accompany you part
of the way?

BERENGER: [*to* JEAN, *and pointing to the* WAITRESS *who goes back
into the café.*] I asked for mineral water. She's made a mistake.

[JEAN, *scornful and disbelieving, shrugs his shoulders.*]

HOUSEWIFE: [*to the* OLD GENTLEMAN] My husband's waiting for me, thank you. Perhaps some other time . . .

OLD GENTLEMAN: [*to the* HOUSEWIFE] I sincerely hope so, Madame.

HOUSEWIFE: [*to the* OLD GENTLEMAN] So do I! [*She gives him a sweet look as she leaves left.*]

BERENGER: The dust's settled . . .

[JEAN *shrugs his shoulders again.*]

OLD GENTLEMAN: [*to the* LOGICIAN, *and looking after the* HOUSEWIFE] Delightful creature!

JEAN: [*to* BERENGER] A rhinoceros! I can't get over it!

[*The* OLD GENTLEMAN *and the* LOGICIAN *move slowly right and off. They chat amiably.*]

OLD GENTLEMAN: [*to the* LOGICIAN, *after casting a last fond look after the* HOUSEWIFE] Charming, isn't she?

LOGICIAN: [*to the* OLD GENTLEMAN] I'm going to explain to you what a syllogism is.

OLD GENTLEMAN: Ah yes, a syllogism.

JEAN: [*to* BERENGER] I can't get over it! It's unthinkable!

[BERENGER *yawns.*]

LOGICIAN: A syllogism consists of a main proposition, a secondary one, and a conclusion.

OLD GENTLEMAN: What conclusion?

[*The* LOGICIAN *and the* OLD GENTLEMAN *go out.*]

JEAN: I just can't get over it.

BERENGER: Yes, I can see you can't. Well, it was a rhinoceros—all right, so it was a rhinoceros! It's miles away by now . . . miles away . . .

JEAN: But you must see it's fantastic! A rhinoceros loose in the town, and you don't bat an eyelid! It shouldn't be allowed!

[BERENGER *yawns.*]

Put your hand in front of your mouth!

BERENGER: Yais . . . yais . . . It shouldn't be allowed. It's dangerous. I hadn't realized. But don't worry about it, it won't get us here.

JEAN: We ought to protest to the Town Council! What's the Council there for?

BERENGER: [*yawning, then quickly putting his hand to his mouth*] Oh excuse me ... perhaps the rhinoceros escaped from the zoo.

JEAN: You're day-dreaming.

BERENGER: But I'm wide awake.

JEAN: Awake or asleep, it's the same thing.

BERENGER: But there is some difference.

JEAN: That's not the point.

BERENGER: But you just said being awake and being asleep were the same thing ...

JEAN: You didn't understand. There's no difference between dreaming awake and dreaming asleep.

BERENGER: I do dream. Life is a dream.

JEAN: You're certainly dreaming when you say the rhinoceros escaped from the zoo ...

BERENGER: I only said: perhaps.

JEAN: ... because there's been no zoo in our town since the animals were destroyed in the plague ... ages ago ...

BERENGER: [*with the same indifference*] Then perhaps it came from a circus.

JEAN: What circus are you talking about?

BERENGER: I don't know ... some travelling circus.

JEAN: You know perfectly well that the Council banned all travelling performers from the district ... There haven't been any since we were children.

BERENGER: [*trying unsuccessfully to stop yawning*] In that case, maybe it's been hiding ever since in the surrounding swamps?

JEAN: The surrounding swamps! The surrounding swamps! My poor friend, you live in a thick haze of alcohol.

BERENGER: [*naïvely*] That's very true ... it seems to mount from my stomach ...

JEAN: It's clouding your brain! Where do you know of any surrounding swamps? Our district is known as 'little Castille' because the land is so arid.

BERENGER: [*surfeited and pretty weary*] How do I know, then?

Perhaps it's been hiding under a stone? ... Or maybe it's been nesting on some withered branch?

JEAN: If you think you're being witty, you're very much mistaken! You're just being a bore with ... with your stupid paradoxes. You're incapable of talking seriously!

BERENGER: Today, yes, only today ... because of ... because of ... [*He indicates his head with a vague gesture.*]

JEAN: Today the same as any other day!

BERENGER: Oh, not quite as much.

JEAN: Your witticisms are not very inspired.

BERENGER: I wasn't trying to be ...

JEAN: [*interrupting him*] I can't bear people to try and make fun of me!

BERENGER: [*hand on his heart*] But my dear Jean, I'd never allow myself to ...

JEAN: [*interrupting him*] My dear Berenger, you are allowing yourself ...

BERENGER: Oh no, never. I'd never allow myself to.

JEAN: Yes, you would; you've just done so.

BERENGER: But how could you possibly think ...

JEAN: [*interrupting him*] I think what is true!

BERENGER: But I assure you ...

JEAN: [*interrupting him*] ... that you were making fun of me!

BERENGER: You really can be obstinate, sometimes.

JEAN: And now you're calling me a mule into the bargain. Even you must see how insulting you're being.

BERENGER: It would never have entered my mind.

JEAN: You have no mind!

BERENGER: All the more reason why it would never enter it.

JEAN: There are certain things which enter the minds of even people without one.

BERENGER: That's impossible.

JEAN: And why, pray, is it impossible?

BERENGER: Because it's impossible.

JEAN: Then kindly explain to me why it's impossible, as you seem to imagine you can explain everything.

BERENGER: I don't imagine anything of the kind.

JEAN: Then why do you act as if you do? And, I repeat, why are you being so insulting to me?

BERENGER: I'm not insulting you. Far from it. You know what tremendous respect I have for you.

JEAN: In that case, why do you contradict me, making out that it's not dangerous to let a rhinoceros go racing about in the middle of the town—particularly on a Sunday morning when the streets are full of children . . . and adults, too . . .

BERENGER: A lot of them are in church. They don't run any risk . . .

JEAN: [*interrupting him*] If you will allow me to finish . . . and at market time, too.

BERENGER: I never said it wasn't dangerous to let a rhinoceros go racing about the town. I simply said I'd personally never considered the danger. It had never crossed my mind.

JEAN: You never consider anything.

BERENGER: All right, I agree. A rhinoceros roaming about is not a good thing.

JEAN: It shouldn't be allowed.

BERENGER: I agree. It shouldn't be allowed. It's a ridiculous thing all right! But it's no reason for you and me to quarrel. Why go on at me just because some wretched perissodactyle happens to pass by. A stupid quadruped not worth talking about. And ferocious into the bargain. And which has already disappeared, which doesn't exist any longer. We're not going to bother about some animal that doesn't exist. Let's talk about something else, Jean, please; [*He yawns.*] there are plenty of other subjects for conversation. [*He takes his glass:*] To you!

> [*At this moment the* LOGICIAN *and the* OLD GENTLEMAN *come back on stage from left; they walk over, talking as they go, to one of the tables on the café terrace, some distance from* BERENGER *and* JEAN, *behind and to the right of them.*]

JEAN: Put that glass back on the table! You're not to drink it.

> [JEAN *takes a large swallow from his own pastis and puts back the glass, half-empty, on the table.* BERENGER *continues to hold his*

glass, without putting it down, and without daring to drink from it either.]

BERENGER: [*timidly*] There's no point in leaving it for the proprietor. [*He makes as if to drink.*]

JEAN: Put it down, I tell you!

BERENGER: Very well.

[*He is putting the glass back on the table when* DAISY *passes. She is a young blonde typist and she crosses the stage from right to left. When he sees her,* BERENGER *rises abruptly, and in doing so makes an awkward movement; the glass falls and splashes* JEAN'S *trousers.*]

Oh, there's Daisy!

JEAN: Look out! How clumsy you are!

BERENGER: That's Daisy . . . I'm so sorry . . . [*He hides himself out of sight of* DAISY.] I don't want her to see me in this state.

JEAN: Your behaviour's unforgivable, absolutely unforgivable!
[*He looks in the direction of* DAISY, *who is just disappearing.*] Why are you afraid of that young girl?

BERENGER: Oh, be quiet, please be quiet!

JEAN: She doesn't look an unpleasant person!

BERENGER: [*coming back to* JEAN, *now that* DAISY *has gone*] I must apologize once more for . . .

JEAN: You see what comes of drinking, you can no longer control your movements, you've no strength left in your hands, you're besotted and fagged out. You're digging your own grave, my friend, you're destroying yourself.

BERENGER: I don't like the taste of alcohol much. And yet if I don't drink, I'm done for; it's as if I'm frightened, and so I drink not to be frightened any longer.

JEAN: Frightened of what?

BERENGER: I don't know exactly. It's a sort of anguish difficult to describe. I feel out of place in life, among people, and so I take to drink. That calms me down and relaxes me so I can forget.

JEAN: You try to escape from yourself!

BERENGER: I'm so tired, I've been tired for years. It's exhausting to drag the weight of my own body about . . .

JEAN: That's alcoholic neurasthenia, drinker's gloom . . .

BERENGER: [*continuing*] I'm conscious of my body all the time, as if it were made of lead, or as if I were carrying another man around on my back. I can't seem to get used to myself. I don't even know if I *am* me. Then as soon as I take a drink, the lead slips away and I recognize myself, I become me again.

JEAN: That's just being fanciful. Look at me, Berenger, I weigh more than you do. And yet I feel light, light as a feather! [*He flaps his arms as if about to fly. The* OLD GENTLEMAN *and the* LOGICIAN *have come back and have taken a few steps on stage deep in talk. At this moment they are passing by* JEAN *and* BERENGER. JEAN's *arm deals the* OLD GENTLEMAN *a sharp knock which precipitates him into the arms of the* LOGICIAN.]

LOGICIAN: An example of a syllogism . . . [*He is knocked.*] Oh!

OLD GENTLEMAN: [*to* JEAN] Look out! [*To the* LOGICIAN:] I'm so sorry.

JEAN: [*to the* OLD GENTLEMAN] I'm so sorry.

LOGICIAN: [*to the* OLD GENTLEMAN] No harm done.

OLD GENTLEMAN: [*to* JEAN] No harm done.

    [*The* OLD GENTLEMAN *and the* LOGICIAN *go and sit at one of the terrace tables a little to the right and behind* JEAN *and* BERENGER.]

BERENGER: [*to* JEAN] You certainly are strong.

JEAN: Yes, I'm strong. I'm strong for several reasons. In the first place I'm strong because I'm naturally strong, and secondly I'm strong because I have moral strength. I'm also strong because I'm not riddled with alcohol. I don't wish to offend you, my dear Berenger, but I feel I must tell you that it's alcohol which weighs so heavy on you.

LOGICIAN: [*to the* OLD GENTLEMAN] Here is an example of a syllogism. The cat has four paws. Isidore and Fricot both have four paws. Therefore Isidore and Fricot are cats.

OLD GENTLEMAN: [*to the* LOGICIAN] My dog has got four paws.

LOGICIAN: [*to the* OLD GENTLEMAN] Then it's a cat.

BERENGER: [*to* JEAN] I've barely got the strength to go on living. Maybe I don't even want to.

OLD GENTLEMAN: [*to the* LOGICIAN, *after deep reflection*] So then logically speaking, my dog must be a cat?

LOGICIAN: [*to the* OLD GENTLEMAN] Logically, yes. But the contrary is also true.

BERENGER: [*to* JEAN] Solitude seems to oppress me. And so does the company of other people.

JEAN: [*to* BERENGER] You contradict yourself. What oppresses you—solitude, or the company of others? You consider yourself a thinker, yet you're devoid of logic.

OLD GENTLEMAN: [*to the* LOGICIAN] Logic is a very beautiful thing.

LOGICIAN: [*to the* OLD GENTLEMAN] As long as it is not abused.

BERENGER: [*to* JEAN] Life is an abnormal business.

JEAN: On the contrary. Nothing could be more natural, and the proof is that people go on living.

BERENGER: There are more dead people than living. And their numbers are increasing. The living are getting rarer.

JEAN: The dead don't exist, there's no getting away from that! ... Ah! Ah ... ! [*He gives a huge laugh.*] Yet you're oppressed by them, too? How can you be oppressed by something that doesn't exist?

BERENGER: I sometimes wonder if I exist myself.

JEAN: You don't exist, my dear Berenger, because you don't think. Start thinking, then you will.

LOGICIAN: [*to the* OLD GENTLEMAN] Another syllogism. All cats die. Socrates is dead. Therefore Socrates is a cat.

OLD GENTLEMAN: And he's got four paws. That's true. I've got a cat named Socrates.

LOGICIAN: There you are, you see ...

JEAN: [*to* BERENGER] Fundamentally you're just a bluffer. And a liar. You say that life doesn't interest you. And yet there's somebody who does.

BERENGER: Who?

JEAN: Your little friend from the office who just went past. You're very fond of her!

OLD GENTLEMAN: [*to the* LOGICIAN] So Socrates was a cat, was he?

LOGICIAN: Logic has just revealed the fact to us.

JEAN: [to BERENGER] You didn't want her to see you in your present state. [BERENGER makes a gesture.] That proves you're not indifferent to everything. But how can you expect Daisy to be attracted to a drunkard?

LOGICIAN: [to the OLD GENTLEMAN] Let's get back to our cats.

OLD GENTLEMAN: [to the LOGICIAN] I'm all ears.

BERENGER: [to JEAN] In any case, I think she's already got her eye on someone.

JEAN: Oh, who?

BERENGER: Dudard. An office colleague, qualified in law, with a big future in the firm—and in Daisy's affections. I can't hope to compete with him.

LOGICIAN: [to the OLD GENTLEMAN] The cat Isidore has four paws.

OLD GENTLEMAN: How do you know?

LOGICIAN: It's stated in the hypothesis.

BERENGER: [to JEAN] The Chief thinks a lot of him. Whereas I've no future, I've no qualifications. I don't stand a chance.

OLD GENTLEMAN: [to the LOGICIAN] Ah! In the hypothesis.

JEAN: [to BERENGER] So you're giving up, just like that . . . ?

BERENGER: What else can I do?

LOGICIAN: [to the OLD GENTLEMAN] Fricot also has four paws. So how many paws have Fricot and Isidore?

OLD GENTLEMAN: Separately or together?

JEAN: [to BERENGER] Life is a struggle, it's cowardly not to put up a fight!

LOGICIAN: [to the OLD GENTLEMAN] Separately or together, it all depends.

BERENGER: [to JEAN] What can I do? I've nothing to put up a fight with.

JEAN: Then find yourself some weapons, my friend.

OLD GENTLEMAN: [to the LOGICIAN, after painful reflection] Eight, eight paws.

LOGICIAN: Logic involves mental arithmetic, you see.

OLD GENTLEMAN: It certainly has many aspects!

BERENGER: [to JEAN] Where can I find the weapons?

LOGICIAN: [*to the* OLD GENTLEMAN] There are no limits to logic.

JEAN: Within yourself. Through your own will.

BERENGER: What weapons?

LOGICIAN: [*to the* OLD GENTLEMAN] I'm going to show you . . .

JEAN: [*to* BERENGER] The weapons of patience and culture, the weapons of the mind. [BERENGER *yawns*.] Turn yourself into a keen and brilliant intellect. Get yourself up to the mark!

BERENGER: How do I get myself up to the mark?

LOGICIAN: [*to the* OLD GENTLEMAN] If I take two paws away from these cats—how many does each have left?

OLD GENTLEMAN: That's not so easy.

BERENGER: [*to* JEAN] That's not so easy.

LOGICIAN: [*to the* OLD GENTLEMAN] On the contrary, it's simple.

OLD GENTLEMAN: [*to the* LOGICIAN] It may be simple for you, but not for me.

BERENGER: [*to* JEAN] It may be simple for you, but not for me.

LOGICIAN: [*to the* OLD GENTLEMAN] Come on, exercise your mind. Concentrate!

JEAN: [*to* BERENGER] Come on, exercise your will. Concentrate!

OLD GENTLEMAN: [*to the* LOGICIAN] I don't see how.

BERENGER: [*to* JEAN] I really don't see how.

LOGICIAN: [*to the* OLD GENTLEMAN] You have to be told everything.

JEAN: [*to* BERENGER] You have to be told everything.

LOGICIAN: [*to the* OLD GENTLEMAN] Take a sheet of paper and calculate. If you take six paws from the two cats, how many paws are left to each cat?

OLD GENTLEMAN: Just a moment . . . [*He calculates on a sheet of paper which he takes from his pocket.*]

JEAN: This is what you must do: dress yourself properly, shave every day, put on a clean shirt.

BERENGER: The laundry's so expensive . . .

JEAN: Cut down on your drinking. This is the way to come out: wear a hat, a tie like this, a well-cut suit, shoes well polished. [*As he mentions the various items of clothing he points self-contentedly to his own hat, tie and shoes.*]

OLD GENTLEMAN: [*to the* LOGICIAN] There are several possible solutions.

LOGICIAN: [*to the* OLD GENTLEMAN] Tell me.

BERENGER: [*to* JEAN] Then what do I do? Tell me . . .

LOGICIAN: [*to the* OLD GENTLEMAN] I'm listening.

BERENGER: [*to* JEAN] I'm listening.

JEAN: You're a timid creature, but not without talent.

BERENGER: I've got talent, me?

JEAN: So use it. Put yourself in the picture. Keep abreast of the cultural and literary events of the times.

OLD GENTLEMAN: [*to the* LOGICIAN] One possibility is: one cat could have four paws and the other two.

BERENGER: [*to* JEAN] I get so little spare time!

LOGICIAN: [*to the* OLD GENTLEMAN] You're not without talent. You just needed to exercise it.

JEAN: Take advantage of what free time you *do* have. Don't just let yourself drift.

OLD GENTLEMAN: I've never had the time. I was an official, you know.

LOGICIAN: One can always find time to learn.

JEAN: [*to* BERENGER] One can always find time.

BERENGER: [*to* JEAN] It's too late now.

OLD GENTLEMAN: [*to the* LOGICIAN] It's a bit late in the day for me.

JEAN: [*to* BERENGER] It's never too late.

LOGICIAN: [*to the* OLD GENTLEMAN] It's never too late.

JEAN: [*to* BERENGER] You work eight hours a day, like me and everybody else, but not on Sundays, nor in the evening, nor for three weeks in the summer. That's quite sufficient, with a little method.

LOGICIAN: [*to the* OLD GENTLEMAN] Well, what about the other solutions? Use a little method, a little method!

[*The* OLD GENTLEMAN *starts to calculate anew.*]

JEAN: [*to* BERENGER] Look, instead of drinking and feeling sick, isn't it better to be fresh and eager, even at work? And you can spend your free time constructively.

BERENGER: How do you mean?

JEAN: By visiting museums, reading literary periodicals, going to lectures. That'll solve your troubles, it will develop your mind. In four weeks you'll be a cultured man.

BERENGER: You're right!

OLD GENTLEMAN: [*to the* LOGICIAN] There could be one cat with five paws . . .

JEAN: [*to* BERENGER] You see, you even think so yourself!

OLD GENTLEMAN: [*to the* LOGICIAN] And one cat with one paw. But would they still be cats, then?

LOGICIAN: [*to the* OLD GENTLEMAN] Why not?

JEAN: [*to* BERENGER] Instead of squandering all your spare money on drink, isn't it better to buy a ticket for an interesting play? Do you know anything about the avant-garde theatre there's so much talk about? Have you seen Ionesco's plays?

BERENGER: [*to* JEAN] Unfortunately, no. I've only heard people talk about them.

OLD GENTLEMAN: [*to the* LOGICIAN] By taking two of the eight paws away from the two cats . . .

JEAN: [*to* BERENGER] There's one playing now. Take advantage of it.

OLD GENTLEMAN: [*to the* LOGICIAN] . . . we could have one cat with six paws . . .

BERENGER: It would be an excellent initiation into the artistic life of our times.

OLD GENTLEMAN: [*to the* LOGICIAN] We could have one cat with no paws at all.

BERENGER: You're right, perfectly right. I'm going to put myself into the picture, like you said.

LOGICIAN: [*to the* OLD GENTLEMAN] In that case, one cat would be specially privileged.

BERENGER: [*to* JEAN] I will, I promise you.

JEAN: You promise yourself, that's the main thing.

OLD GENTLEMAN: And one under-privileged cat deprived of all paws.

BERENGER: I make myself a solemn promise, I'll keep my word to myself.

LOGICIAN: That would be unjust, and therefore not logical.

BERENGER: Instead of drinking, I'll develop my mind. I feel better already. My head already feels clearer.

JEAN: You see!

OLD GENTLEMAN: [*to the* LOGICIAN] Not logical?

BERENGER: This afternoon I'll go to the museum. And I'll book two seats for the theatre this evening. Will you come with me?

LOGICIAN: [*to the* OLD GENTLEMAN] Because Logic means Justice.

JEAN: [*to* BERENGER] You must persevere. Keep up your good resolutions.

OLD GENTLEMAN: [*to the* LOGICIAN] I get it. Justice . . .

BERENGER: [*to* JEAN] I promise you, and I promise myself. Will you come to the museum with me this afternoon?

JEAN: [*to* BERENGER] I have to take a rest this afternoon; it's in my programme for the day.

OLD GENTLEMAN: Justice is one more aspect of Logic.

BERENGER: [*to* JEAN] But you will come with me to the theatre this evening?

JEAN: No, not this evening.

LOGICIAN: [*to the* OLD GENTLEMAN] Your mind is getting clearer!

JEAN: [*to* BERENGER] I sincerely hope you'll keep up your good resolutions. But this evening I have to meet some friends for a drink.

BERENGER: For a drink?

OLD GENTLEMAN: [*to the* LOGICIAN] What's more, a cat with no paws at all . . .

JEAN: [*to* BERENGER] I've promised to go. I always keep my word.

OLD GENTLEMAN: [*to the* LOGICIAN] . . . wouldn't be able to run fast enough to catch mice.

BERENGER: [*to* JEAN] Ah, now it's you that's setting me a bad example! You're going out drinking.

LOGICIAN: [*to the* OLD GENTLEMAN] You're already making progress in logic.

[*A sound of rapid galloping is heard approaching again, trumpeting and the sound of rhinoceros hooves and pantings; this time the*

*sound comes from the opposite direction approaching from back-
stage to front, in the left wings.*]

JEAN: [*furiously to* BERENGER] It's not a habit with me, you know.
It's not the same as with you. With you . . . you're . . . it's not
the same thing at all . . .

BERENGER: Why isn't it the same thing?

JEAN: [*shouting over the noise coming from the café*] I'm no drunkard,
not me!

LOGICIAN: [*shouting to the* OLD GENTLEMAN] Even with no paws
a cat must catch mice. That's in it's nature.

BERENGER: [*shouting very loudly*] I didn't mean you were a
drunkard. But why would it make me one any more than you,
in a case like that?

OLD GENTLEMAN: [*shouting to the* LOGICIAN] What's in the cat's
nature?

JEAN: [*to* BERENGER] Because there's moderation in all things. I'm
a moderate person, not like you!

LOGICIAN: [*to the* OLD GENTLEMAN, *cupping his hands to his ears*]
What did you say? [*Deafening sounds drown the words of the
four characters.*]

BERENGER: [*to* JEAN, *cupping his hands to his ears*] What about me,
what? What did you say?

JEAN: [*roaring*] I said that . . .

OLD GENTLEMAN: [*roaring*] I said that . . .

JEAN: [*suddenly aware of the noises which are now very near*] Whatever's happening?

LOGICIAN: What is going on?

JEAN: [*rises, knocking his chair over as he does so; looks towards left
wings where the noises of the passing rhinoceros are coming from*]
Oh, a rhinoceros!

LOGICIAN: [*rising, knocking over his chair*] Oh, a rhinoceros!

OLD GENTLEMAN: [*doing the same*] Oh, a rhinoceros!

BERENGER: [*still seated, but this time, taking more notice*] Rhinoceros!
In the opposite direction!

WAITRESS: [*emerging with a tray and glasses*] What is it? Oh, a
rhinoceros! [*She drops the tray, breaking the glasses.*]

PROPRIETOR: [*coming out of the café*] What's going on?

WAITRESS: [*to the* PROPRIETOR] A rhinoceros!

LOGICIAN: A rhinoceros, going full-tilt on the opposite pavement!

GROCER: [*coming out of his shop*] Oh, a rhinoceros!

JEAN: Oh, a rhinoceros!

GROCER'S WIFE: [*sticking her head through the upstairs window of shop*] Oh, a rhinoceros!

PROPRIETOR: It's no reason to break the glasses.

JEAN: It's rushing straight ahead, brushing up against the shop windows.

DAISY: [*entering left*] Oh, a rhinoceros!

BERENGER: [*noticing* DAISY] Oh, Daisy!

[*Noise of people fleeing, the same 'Ohs' and 'Ahs' as before.*]

WAITRESS: Well, of all things!

PROPRIETOR: [*to the* WAITRESS] You'll be charged up for those!

[BERENGER *tries to make himself scarce, not to be seen by* DAISY. *The* OLD GENTLEMAN, *the* LOGICIAN, *the* GROCER *and his* WIFE *move to centre-stage and say together:*]

ALL: Well, of all things!

JEAN and
BERENGER: Well, of all things!

[*A piteous mewing is heard, then an equally piteous cry of a woman.*]

ALL: Oh!

[*Almost at the same time, and as the noises are rapidly dying away the* HOUSEWIFE *appears without her basket but holding the blood-stained corpse of her cat in her arms.*]

HOUSEWIFE: [*wailing*] It ran over my cat, it ran over my cat!

WAITRESS: It ran over her cat!

[*The* GROCER, *his* WIFE (*at the window*), *the* OLD GENTLEMAN, DAISY *and the* LOGICIAN *crowd round the* HOUSEWIFE, *saying:*]

ALL: What a tragedy, poor little thing!

OLD GENTLEMAN: Poor little thing!

DAISY and
WAITRESS: Poor little thing!

GROCER'S WIFE: [*at the window*]
OLD GENTLEMAN: } Poor little thing!
LOGICIAN:

PROPRIETOR: [*to the* WAITRESS, *pointing to the broken glasses and the upturned chairs*] Don't just stand there! Clear up the mess!
>[JEAN *and* BERENGER *also rush over to the* HOUSEWIFE *who continues to lament, her dead cat in her arms.*]

WAITRESS: [*moving to the café terrace to pick up the broken glasses and the chairs, and looking over her shoulder at the* HOUSEWIFE] Oh, poor little thing!

PROPRIETOR: [*pointing, for the* WAITRESS'S *benefit, to the debris*] Over there, over there!

OLD GENTLEMAN: [*to the* GROCER] Well, what do you think of that?

BERENGER: [*to the* HOUSEWIFE] You mustn't cry like that, it's too heartbreaking!

DAISY: [*to* BERENGER] Were you there, Mr. Berenger? Did you see it?

BERENGER: [*to* DAISY] Good morning, Miss Daisy, you must excuse me, I haven't had a chance to shave . . .

PROPRIETOR: [*supervising the clearing up of the debris, then glancing towards the* HOUSEWIFE] Poor little thing!

WAITRESS: [*clearing up the mess, her back to the* HOUSEWIFE] Poor little thing!
>[*These remarks must obviously be made very rapidly, almost simultaneously.*]

GROCER'S WIFE: [*at window*] That's going too far!

JEAN: That's going too far!

HOUSEWIFE: [*lamenting, and cradling the dead cat in her arms*] My poor little pussy, my poor little cat.

OLD GENTLEMAN: [*to the* HOUSEWIFE] What can you do, dear lady, cats are only mortal.

LOGICIAN: What do you expect, Madame? All cats are mortal! One must accept that.

HOUSEWIFE: [*lamenting*] My little cat, my poor little cat.

PROPRIETOR: [*to the* WAITRESS *whose apron is full of broken glass*]

Throw that in the dustbin! [*He has picked up the chairs.*] You owe me a thousand francs.

WAITRESS: [*moving into the café*] All you think of is money!

GROCER'S WIFE: [*to the* HOUSEWIFE; *from window*] Don't upset yourself!

OLD GENTLEMAN: [*to the* HOUSEWIFE] Don't upset yourself, dear lady!

GROCER'S WIFE: [*from window*] It's very upsetting a thing like that!

HOUSEWIFE: My little cat, my little cat!

DAISY: Yes, it's very upsetting a thing like that.

OLD GENTLEMAN: [*supporting the* HOUSEWIFE, *and guiding her to a table on the terrace followed by the others*] Sit down here, dear lady.

JEAN: [*to the* OLD GENTLEMAN] Well, what do you think of that?

GROCER: [*to the* LOGICIAN] Well, what do you think of that?

GROCER'S WIFE: [*to* DAISY, *from window*] Well, what do you think of that?

PROPRIETOR: [*to the* WAITRESS, *who comes back while they are installing the weeping* HOUSEWIFE *at one of the terrace tables, still cradling her dead cat.*] A glass of water for the lady.

OLD GENTLEMAN: [*to the* HOUSEWIFE] Sit down, dear lady!

JEAN: Poor woman!

GROCER'S WIFE: [*from window*] Poor cat!

BERENGER: [*to the* WAITRESS] Better give her a brandy.

PROPRIETOR: [*to the* WAITRESS] A brandy! [*Pointing to* BERENGER:] This gentleman is paying!

WAITRESS: [*going into the café*] One brandy, right away!

HOUSEWIFE: [*sobbing*] I don't want any, I don't want any!

GROCER: It went past my shop a little while ago.

JEAN: [*to the* GROCER] It wasn't the same one!

GROCER: [*to* JEAN] But I could have . . .

GROCER'S WIFE: Yes it was, it was the same one.

DAISY: Did it go past twice, then?

PROPRIETOR: I think it was the same one.

JEAN: No, it was not the same rhinoceros. The one that went by first had two horns on its nose, it was an Asiatic rhinoceros; this only had one, it was an African rhinoceros!

[*The* WAITRESS *appears with a glass of brandy and takes it to the* HOUSEWIFE.]

OLD GENTLEMAN: Here's a drop of brandy to pull you together.

HOUSEWIFE: [*in tears*] No . . . o . . . o . . .

BERENGER: [*suddenly unnerved, to* JEAN] You're talking nonsense . . . How could you possibly tell about the horns? The animal flashed past at such speed, we hardly even saw it . . .

DAISY: [*to the* HOUSEWIFE] Go on, it will do you good!

OLD GENTLEMAN: [*to* BERENGER] Very true. It did go fast.

PROPRIETOR: [*to the* HOUSEWIFE] Just have a taste, it's good.

BERENGER: [*to* JEAN] You had no time to count its horns . . .

GROCER'S WIFE: [*to the* WAITRESS, *from window*] Make her drink it.

BERENGER: [*to* JEAN] What's more, it was travelling in a cloud of dust.

DAISY: [*to the* HOUSEWIFE] Drink it up.

OLD GENTLEMAN: [*to the* HOUSEWIFE] Just a sip, dear little lady . . . be brave . . .

[*The* WAITRESS *forces her to drink it by putting the glass to her lips; the* HOUSEWIFE *feigns refusal, but drinks all the same.*]

WAITRESS: There, you see!

GROCER'S WIFE: [*from her window*]

and DAISY: There, you see!

JEAN: [*to* BERENGER] I don't have to grope my way through a fog. I can calculate quickly, my mind is clear!

OLD GENTLEMAN: [*to the* HOUSEWIFE] Better now?

BERENGER: [*to* JEAN] But it had its head thrust down.

PROPRIETOR: [*to the* HOUSEWIFE] Now wasn't that good?

JEAN: [*to* BERENGER] Precisely, one could see all the better.

HOUSEWIFE: [*after having drunk*] My little cat!

BERENGER: [*irritated*] Utter nonsense!

GROCER'S WIFE: [*to the* HOUSEWIFE, *from window*] I've got another cat you can have.

JEAN: [*to* BERENGER] What me? You dare to accuse me of talking nonsense?

HOUSEWIFE: [*to the* GROCER'S WIFE] I'll never have another! [*She weeps, cradling her cat.*]

BERENGER: [*to* JEAN] Yes, absolute, blithering nonsense!

PROPRIETOR: [*to the* HOUSEWIFE] You have to accept these things!

JEAN: [*to* BERENGER] I've never talked nonsense in my life!

OLD GENTLEMAN: [*to the* HOUSEWIFE] Try and be philosophic about it!

BERENGER: [*to* JEAN] You're just a pretentious show-off—[*Raising his voice:*] a pedant!

PROPRIETOR: [*to* JEAN *and* BERENGER] Now, gentlemen!

BERENGER: [*to* JEAN, *continuing*] . . . and what's more, a pedant who's not certain of his facts because in the first place it's the Asiatic rhinoceros with only one horn on its nose, and it's the African with two . . .

> [*The other characters leave the* HOUSEWIFE *and crowd round* JEAN *and* BERENGER *who argue at the top of their voices.*]

JEAN: [*to* BERENGER] You're wrong, it's the other way about!

HOUSEWIFE: [*left alone*] He was so sweet!

BERENGER: Do you want to bet?

WAITRESS: They want to make a bet!

DAISY: [*to* BERENGER] Don't excite yourself, Mr. Berenger.

JEAN: [*to* BERENGER] I'm not betting with you. If anybody's got two horns, it's you! You Asiatic Mongol!

WAITRESS: Oh!

GROCER'S WIFE: [*from window to her husband*] They're going to have a fight!

GROCER: [*to his* WIFE] Nonsense, it's just a bet!

PROPRIETOR: [*to* JEAN *and* BERENGER] We don't want any scenes here!

OLD GENTLEMAN: Now look . . . What kind of rhinoceros has one horn on its nose? [*To the* GROCER:] You're a tradesman, you should know.

GROCER'S WIFE: [*to her husband*] Yes, you should know!

BERENGER: [*to* JEAN] I've got no horns. And I never will have.

GROCER: [*to the* OLD GENTLEMAN] Tradesmen can't be expected to know everything.

JEAN: [*to* BERENGER] Oh yes, you have!

BERENGER: [*to* JEAN] I'm not Asiatic either. And in any case, Asiatics are people the same as everyone else . . .

WAITRESS: Yes, Asiatics are people the same as we are . . .

OLD GENTLEMAN: [*to the* PROPRIETOR] That's true!

PROPRIETOR: [*to the* WAITRESS] Nobody's asking for your opinion!

DAISY: [*to the* PROPRIETOR] She's right. They're people the same as we are.

[*The* HOUSEWIFE *continues to lament throughout this discussion.*]

HOUSEWIFE: He was so gentle, just like one of us.

JEAN: [*beside himself*] They're yellow!

[*The* LOGICIAN, *a little to one side between the* HOUSEWIFE *and the group which has formed round* JEAN *and* BERENGER, *follows the controversy attentively, without taking part.*]

Good-bye gentlemen! [*To* BERENGER:] You, I will not deign to include!

HOUSEWIFE: He was devoted to us! [*She sobs.*]

DAISY: Now listen a moment, Mr. Berenger, and you, too, Mr. Jean . . .

OLD GENTLEMAN: I once had some friends who were Asiatics! But perhaps they weren't real ones . . .

PROPRIETOR: I've known some real ones.

WAITRESS: [*to the* GROCER'S WIFE] I had an Asiatic friend once.

HOUSEWIFE: [*still sobbing*] I had him when he was a little kitten.

JEAN: [*still quite beside himself*] They're yellow, I tell you, bright yellow!

BERENGER: [*to* JEAN] Whatever they are, you're bright red!

GROCER'S WIFE: [*from window*]

and WAITRESS: Oh!

PROPRIETOR: This is getting serious!

HOUSEWIFE: He was so clean. He always used his tray.

JEAN: [*to* BERENGER] If that's how you feel, it's the last time you'll see me. I'm not wasting my time with a fool like you.

HOUSEWIFE: He always made himself understood.

[JEAN *goes off right, very fast and furious . . . but doubles back before making his final exit.*]

OLD GENTLEMAN: [*to the* GROCER] There are white Asiatics as well, and black and blue, and even some like us.

JEAN: [*to* BERENGER] You drunkard!

[*Everybody looks at him in consternation.*]

BERENGER: [*to* JEAN] I'm not going to stand for that!

ALL: [*looking in* JEAN'S *direction*] Oh!

HOUSEWIFE: He could almost talk—in fact he did.

DAISY: [*to* BERENGER] You shouldn't have made him angry.

BERENGER: [*to* DAISY] It wasn't my fault.

PROPRIETOR: [*to the* WAITRESS] Go and get a little coffin for the poor thing . . .

OLD GENTLEMAN: [*to* BERENGER] I think you're right. It's the Asiatic rhinoceros with two horns and the African with one . . .

GROCER: But he was saying the opposite.

DAISY: [*to* BERENGER] You were both wrong!

OLD GENTLEMAN: [*to* BERENGER] Even so, you were right.

WAITRESS: [*to the* HOUSEWIFE] Come with me, we're going to put him in a little box.

HOUSEWIFE: [*sobbing desperately*] No, never!

GROCER: If you don't mind my saying so, I think Mr. Jean was right.

DAISY: [*turning to the* HOUSEWIFE] Now, you must be reasonable!

[DAISY *and the* WAITRESS *lead the* HOUSEWIFE, *with her dead cat, towards the café entrance.*]

OLD GENTLEMAN: [*to* DAISY *and the* WAITRESS] Would you like me to come with you?

GROCER: The Asiatic rhinoceros has one horn and the African rhinoceros has two. And vice versa.

DAISY: [*to the* OLD GENTLEMAN] No, don't you bother.

[DAISY *and the* WAITRESS *enter the café leading the inconsolable* HOUSEWIFE.]

GROCER'S WIFE: [*to the* GROCER, *from window*] Oh you always have to be different from everybody else!

BERENGER: [*aside, whilst the others continue to discuss the horns of the rhinoceros*] Daisy was right, I should never have contradicted him.

PROPRIETOR: [*to the* GROCER'S WIFE] Your husband's right, the Asiatic rhinoceros has two horns and the African one must have two, and vice versa.

BERENGER: [*aside*] He can't stand being contradicted. The slightest disagreement makes him fume.

OLD GENTLEMAN: [*to the* PROPRIETOR] You're mistaken, my friend.

PROPRIETOR: [*to the* OLD GENTLEMAN] I'm very sorry, I'm sure.

BERENGER: [*aside*] His temper's his only fault.

GROCER'S WIFE: [*from window, to the* OLD GENTLEMAN, *the* PROPRIETOR *and the* GROCER] Maybe they're both the same.

BERENGER: [*aside*] Deep down, he's got a heart of gold; he's done me many a good turn.

PROPRIETOR: [*to the* GROCER'S WIFE] If the one has two horns, then the other must have one.

OLD GENTLEMAN: Perhaps it's the other with two and the one with one.

BERENGER: [*aside*] I'm sorry I wasn't more accommodating. But why is he so obstinate? I didn't want to exasperate him. [*To the others:*] He's always making fantastic statements! Always trying to dazzle people with his knowledge. He never will admit he's wrong.

OLD GENTLEMAN: [*to* BERENGER] Have you any proof?

BERENGER: Proof of what?

OLD GENTLEMAN: Of the statement you made just now which started the unfortunate row with your friend.

GROCER: [*to* BERENGER] Yes, have you any proof?

OLD GENTLEMAN: [*to* BERENGER] How do you know that one of the two rhinoceroses has one horn and the other two? And which is which?

GROCER'S WIFE: He doesn't know any more than we do.

BERENGER: In the first place we don't know that there were two. I myself believe there was only one.

PROPRIETOR: Well, let's say there were two. Does the single-horned one come from Asia?

OLD GENTLEMAN: No. It's the one from Africa with two, I think.

PROPRIETOR: Which is two-horned?

GROCER: It's not the one from Africa.

GROCER'S WIFE: It's not easy to agree on this.

OLD GENTLEMAN: But the problem must be cleared up.

LOGICIAN: [*emerging from his isolation*] Excuse me gentlemen for interrupting. But that is not the question. Allow me to introduce myself . . .

HOUSEWIFE: [*coming out of the café in tears*] He's a logician.

PROPRIETOR: Oh! A logician, is he?

OLD GENTLEMAN: [*introducing the* LOGICIAN *to* BERENGER] My friend, the Logician.

BERENGER: Very happy to meet you.

LOGICIAN: [*continuing*] Professional Logician; my card. [*He shows his card.*]

BERENGER: It's a great honour.

GROCER: A great honour for all of us.

PROPRIETOR: Would you mind telling us then, sir, if the African rhinoceros is single-horned . . .

OLD GENTLEMAN: Or bicorned . . .

GROCER'S WIFE: And is the Asiatic rhinoceros bicorned . . .

GROCER: Or unicorned.

LOGICIAN: Exactly, that is not the question. Let me make myself clear.

GROCER: But it's still what we want to find out.

LOGICIAN: Kindly allow me to speak, gentlemen.

OLD GENTLEMAN: Let him speak!

GROCER'S WIFE: [*to the* GROCER, *from window*] Give him a chance to speak.

PROPRIETOR: We're listening, sir.

LOGICIAN: [*to* BERENGER] I'm addressing you in particular. And all the others present as well.

GROCER: Us as well . . .

LOGICIAN: You see, you have got away from the problem which

instigated the debate. In the first place you were deliberating whether or not the rhinoceros which passed by just now was the same one that passed by earlier, or whether it was another. That is the question to decide.

BERENGER: Yes, but how?

LOGICIAN: Thus: you may have seen on two occasions a single rhinoceros bearing a single horn . . .

GROCER: [*repeating the words, as if to understand better*] On two occasions a single rhinoceros . . .

PROPRIETOR: [*doing the same*] Bearing a single horn . . .

LOGICIAN: . . . or you may have seen on two occasions a single rhinoceros with two horns.

OLD GENTLEMAN: [*repeating the words*] A single rhinoceros with two horns on two occasions . . .

LOGICIAN: Exactly. Or again, you may have seen one rhinoceros with one horn, and then another also with a single horn.

GROCER'S WIFE: [*from window*] Ha, ha . . .

LOGICIAN. Or again, an initial rhinoceros with two horns, followed by a second with two horns . . .

PROPRIETOR: That's true.

LOGICIAN: Now, if you had seen . . .

GROCER: If we'd seen . . .

OLD GENTLEMAN: Yes, if we'd seen . . .

LOGICIAN: If on the first occasion you had seen a rhinoceros with two horns . . .

PROPRIETOR: With two horns . . .

LOGICIAN: And on the second occasion, a rhinoceros with one horn . . .

GROCER: With one horn . . .

LOGICIAN: That wouldn't be conclusive either.

OLD GENTLEMAN: Even that wouldn't be conclusive.

PROPRIETOR: Why not?

GROCER'S WIFE: Oh, I don't get it at all.

GROCER: Shoo! Shoo!

[*The* GROCER'S WIFE *shrugs her shoulders and withdraws from her window.*]

LOGICIAN: For it is possible that since its first appearance, the rhinoceros may have lost one of its horns, and that the first and second transit were still made by a single beast.

BERENGER: I see, but . . .

OLD GENTLEMAN: [*interrupting* BERENGER] Don't interrupt!

LOGICIAN: It may also be that two rhinoceroses both with two horns may each have lost a horn.

OLD GENTLEMAN: That is possible.

PROPRIETOR: Yes, that's possible.

GROCER: Why not?

BERENGER: Yes, but in any case . . .

OLD GENTLEMAN: [*to* BERENGER] Don't interrupt.

LOGICIAN: If you could prove that on the first occasion you saw a rhinoceros with one horn, either Asiatic or African . . .

OLD GENTLEMAN: Asiatic or African . . .

LOGICIAN: And on the second occasion a rhinoceros with two horns . . .

GROCER: One with two . . .

LOGICIAN: No matter whether African or Asiatic . . .

OLD GENTLEMAN: African or Asiatic . . .

LOGICIAN: . . . we could then conclude that we were dealing with two different rhinoceroses, for it is hardly likely that a second horn could grow sufficiently in a space of a few minutes to be visible on the nose of a rhinoceros.

OLD GENTLEMAN: It's hardly likely.

LOGICIAN: [*enchanted with his discourse*] That would imply one rhinoceros either Asiatic or African . . .

OLD GENTLEMAN: Asiatic or African . . .

LOGICIAN: . . . and one rhinoceros either African or Asiatic.

PROPRIETOR: African or Asiatic.

GROCER: Er . . . yais.

LOGICIAN: For good logic cannot entertain the possibility that the same creature be born in two places at the same time . . .

OLD GENTLEMAN: Or even successively.

LOGICIAN: [*to* OLD GENTLEMAN] Which was to be proved.

BERENGER: [*to* LOGICIAN] That seems clear enough, but it doesn't answer the question.

LOGICIAN: [*to* BERENGER, *with a knowledgeable smile*] Obviously, my dear sir, but now the problem is correctly posed.

OLD GENTLEMAN: It's quite logical. Quite logical.

LOGICIAN: [*raising his hat*] Good-bye, gentlemen.

[*He retires, going out left, followed by the* OLD GENTLEMAN.]

OLD GENTLEMAN: Good-bye, gentlemen. [*He raises his hat and follows the* LOGICIAN *out.*]

GROCER: Well, it may be logical . . .

[*At this moment the* HOUSEWIFE *comes out of the café in deep mourning, and carrying a box; she is followed by* DAISY *and the* WAITRESS *as if for a funeral. The* cortège *moves towards the right exit.*]

. . . it may be logical, but are we going to stand for our cats being run down under our very eyes by one-horned rhinoceroses *or* two, whether they're Asiatic *or* African? [*He indicates with a theatrical gesture the* cortège *which is just leaving.*]

PROPRIETOR: He's absolutely right! We're not standing for our cats being run down by rhinoceroses or anything else!

GROCER: We're not going to stand for it!

GROCER'S WIFE: [*sticking her head round the shop door, to her husband*] Are you coming in? The customers will be here any minute.

GROCER: [*moving to the shop*] No, we're not standing for it.

BERENGER: I should never have quarrelled with Jean! [*To the* PROPRIETOR:] Get me a brandy! A double!

PROPRIETOR: Coming up! [*He goes into the café for the brandy.*]

BERENGER: [*alone*] I never should have quarrelled with Jean. I shouldn't have got into such a rage!

[*The* PROPRIETOR *comes out carrying a large glass of brandy.*]

I feel too upset to go to the museum. I'll cultivate my mind some other time. [*He takes the glass of brandy and drinks it.*]

CURTAIN

ACT TWO

SCENE ONE

A government office, or the office of a private concern—such as a large firm of law publications. Up-stage centre, a large double door, above which a notice reads: 'Chef du Service'. Up-stage left, near to the Head of the Department's door, stands DAISY's *little table with a typewriter. By the left wall, between a door which leads to the staircase and* DAISY's *table, stands another table on which the time sheets are placed, which the employees sign on arrival. The door leading to the staircase is down-stage left. The top steps of the staircase can be seen, the top of a stair-rail and a small landing. In the foreground, a table with two chairs. On the table: printing proofs, an inkwell, pens; this is the table where* BOTARD *and* BERENGER *work;* BERENGER *will sit on the left chair,* BOTARD *on the right. Near to the right wall, another bigger, rectangular table, also covered with papers, proofs, etc.*

Two more chairs stand at each end of this table—more elegant and imposing chairs. This is the table of DUDARD *and* MR. BOEUF. DUDARD *will sit on the chair next to the wall, the other employees facing him. He acts as Deputy-Head. Between the up-stage door and the right wall, there is a window. If the theatre has an orchestra pit it would be preferable to have simply a window frame in front of the stage, facing the auditorium. In the right-hand corner, up-stage, a coat-stand, on which grey blouses or old coats are hung. The coat-stand could also be placed down-stage, near to the right wall.*

On the walls are rows of books and dusty documents. On the back wall, left, above the shelves, there are signs: 'Jurisprudence', 'Codes'; on the right-hand wall which can be slightly on an angle, the signs read: 'Le Journal Officiel', 'Lois fiscales'. Above the Head of the Department's door a clock registers three minutes past nine.

When the curtain rises, DUDARD *is standing near his chair, his right profile to the auditorium; on the other side of the desk, left profile to the auditorium, is* BOTARD; *between them, also near to the desk, facing the auditorium, stands the Head of the Department;* DAISY *is near to the Chief, a little up-stage of him. She holds some sheets of*

*typing paper. On the table round which the three characters stand, a
large open newspaper lies on the printing proofs.*
*When the curtain rises the characters remain fixed for a few seconds in
position for the first line of dialogue. They make a tableau vivant.
The same effect marks the beginning of the first act.*
*The Head of the Department is about forty, very correctly dressed:
dark blue suit, a rosette of the Legion of Honour, starched collar, black
tie, large brown moustache. He is* MR. PAPILLON.
DUDARD, *thirty-five years old; grey suit; he wears black lustrine
sleeves to protect his coat. He may wear spectacles. He is a quite tall,
young employee with a future. If the Department Head became the
Assistant Director he would take his place:* BOTARD *does not like him.*
BOTARD: *former schoolteacher; short, he has a proud air, and wears a
little white moustache; a brisk sixty year-old:* [he knows everything,
understands everything, judges everything]. *He wears a Basque beret,
and wears a long grey blouse during working hours; spectacles on a
longish nose; a pencil behind his ear; he also wears protective sleeves
at work.*
DAISY: *young blonde.*
Later, MRS. BOEUF; *a large woman of some forty to fifty years old,
tearful, and breathless.*
> [*As the curtain rises, the characters therefore are standing motion-
> less around the table, right; the Chief with index finger pointing
> to the newspaper;* DUDARD, *with his hand extended in* BOTARD'S
> *direction, seems to be saying: 'so you see!'* BOTARD, *hands in the
> pocket of his blouse, wears an incredulous smile and seems to say:
> 'You won't take me in.'* DAISY, *with her typing paper in her
> hand seems, from her look, to be supporting* DUDARD.
>
> *After a few brief seconds,* BOTARD *starts the attack.*]

BOTARD: It's all a lot of made-up nonsense.
DAISY: But I saw it, I saw the rhinoceros!
DUDARD: It's in the paper, in black and white, you can't deny
  that.
BOTARD: [*with an air of the greatest scorn*] Pfff!
DUDARD: It's all here; it's down here in the dead cats column!
  Read it for yourself, Chief.

PAPILLON: 'Yesterday, just before lunch time, in the church square of our town, a cat was trampled to death by a pachyderm.'

DAISY: It wasn't exactly in the church square.

PAPILLON: That's all it says. No other details.

BOTARD: Pfff!

DUDARD: Well, that's clear enough.

BOTARD: I never believe journalists. They're all liars. I don't need them to tell me what to think; I believe what I see with my own eyes. Speaking as a former teacher, I like things to be precise, scientifically valid; I've got a methodical mind.

DUDARD: What's a methodical mind got to do with it?

DAISY: [to BOTARD] I think it's stated very precisely, Mr. Botard.

BOTARD: You call that precise? And what, pray, does it mean by a pachyderm? What does the editor of a dead cats column understand by a pachyderm? He doesn't say. And what does he mean by a cat?

DUDARD: Everybody knows what a cat is.

BOTARD: Does it concern a male cat or a female? What breed was it? And what colour? The colour bar is something I feel strongly about. I hate it.

PAPILLON: What has the colour bar to do with it, Mr. Botard? It's quite beside the point.

BOTARD: Please forgive me, Mr. Papillon. But you can't deny that the colour problem is one of the great stumbling blocks of our time.

DUDARD: I know that, we all know that, but it has nothing to do with . . .

BOTARD: It's not an issue to be dismissed lightly, Mr. Dudard. The course of history has shown that racial prejudice . . .

DUDARD: I tell you it doesn't enter into it.

BOTARD: I'm not so sure.

PAPILLON: The colour bar is not the issue at stake.

BOTARD: One should never miss an occasion to denounce it.

DAISY: But we told you that none of us is in favour of the colour bar. You're obscuring the issue; it's simply a question of a cat being run over by a pachyderm—in this case, a rhinoceros.

BOTARD: I'm a Northerner myself. Southerners have got too much imagination. Perhaps it was merely a flea run over by a mouse. People make mountains out of molehills.

PAPILLON: [*to* DUDARD] Let us try and get things clear. Did you yourself, with your own eyes, see a rhinoceros strolling through the streets of the town?

DAISY: It didn't stroll, it ran.

DUDARD: No, I didn't see it personally. But a lot of very reliable people . . . !

BOTARD: [*interrupting him*] It's obvious they were just making it up. You put too much trust in these journalists; they don't care what they invent to sell their wretched newspapers and please the bosses they serve! And you mean to tell me they've taken you in—you, a qualified man of law! Forgive me for laughing! Ha! Ha! Ha!

DAISY: But I saw it, I saw the rhinoceros. I'd take my oath on it.

BOTARD: Get away with you! And I thought you were a sensible girl!

DAISY: Mr. Botard, I can see straight! And I wasn't the only one; there were plenty of other people watching.

BOTARD: Pfff! They were probably watching something else! A few idlers with nothing to do, work-shy loafers!

DUDARD: It happened yesterday, Sunday.

BOTARD: I work on Sundays as well. I've no time for priests who do their utmost to get you to church, just to prevent you from working, and earning your daily bread by the sweat of your brow.

PAPILLON: [*indignant*] Oh!

BOTARD: I'm sorry, I didn't mean to offend you. The fact that I despise religion doesn't mean I don't esteem it highly. [*To* DAISY:] In any case, do you know what a rhinoceros looks like?

DAISY: It's a . . . it's a very big, ugly animal.

BOTARD: And you pride yourself on your precise thinking! The rhinoceros, my dear young lady . . .

PAPILLON: There's no need to start a lecture on the rhinoceros here. We're not in school.

BOTARD: That's a pity.

[*During these last speeches* BERENGER *is seen climbing the last steps of the staircase; he opens the office door cautiously; as he does so one can read the notice on it:* 'Editions de Droit'.]

PAPILLON: Well! It's gone nine, Miss Daisy; put the time sheets away. Too bad about the late-comers.

[DAISY *goes to the little table, left, on which the time sheets are placed, at the same moment as* BERENGER *enters*.]

BERENGER: [*entering, whilst the others continue their discussion, to* DAISY] Good morning, Miss Daisy. I'm not late, am I?

BOTARD: [*to* DUDARD *and* PAPILLON] I campaign against ignorance wherever I find it . . . !

DAISY: [*to* BERENGER] Hurry up, Mr. Berenger.

BOTARD: . . . in palace or humble hut!

DAISY: [*to* BERENGER] Quick! Sign the time sheet!

BERENGER: Oh thank you! Has the Boss arrived?

DAISY: [*a finger on her lips*] Shh! Yes, he's here.

BERENGER: Here already? [*He hurries to sign the time sheet.*]

BOTARD: [*continuing*] No matter where! Even in printing offices.

PAPILLON: [*to* BOTARD] Mr. Botard, I consider . . .

BERENGER: [*signing the sheet, to* DAISY] But it's not ten past . . .

PAPILLON: [*to* BOTARD] I consider you have gone too far.

DUDARD: [*to* PAPILLON] I think so too, sir.

PAPILLON: [*to* BOTARD] Are you suggesting that Mr. Dudard, my colleague and yours, a law graduate and a first-class employee, is ignorant?

BOTARD: I wouldn't go so far as to say that, but the teaching you get at the university isn't up to what you get at the ordinary schools.

PAPILLON: [*to* DAISY] What about that time sheet?

DAISY: [*to* PAPILLON] Here it is, sir. [*She hands it to him.*]

BOTARD: [*to* DUDARD] There's no clear thinking at the universities, no encouragement for practical observation.

DUDARD: [*to* BOTARD] Oh come now!

BERENGER: [*to* PAPILLON] Good morning, Mr. Papillon. [*He has been making his way to the coat-rack behind the Chief's back and around the group formed by the three characters; there he takes down his working overall or his well-worn coat, and hangs up his street coat in its place; he changes his coat by the coat-rack, then makes his way to his desk, from the drawer of which he takes out his black protective sleeves, etc.*] Morning, Mr. Papillon! Sorry I was almost late. Morning Dudard! Morning, Mr. Botard.

PAPILLON: Well Berenger, did you see the rhinoceros by any chance?

BOTARD: [*to* DUDARD] All you get at the universities are effete intellectuals with no practical knowledge of life.

DUDARD: [*to* BOTARD] Rubbish!

BERENGER: [*continuing to arrange his working equipment with excessive zeal as if to make up for his late arrival; in a natural tone to* PAPILLON] Oh yes, I saw it all right.

BOTARD: [*turning round*] Pfff!

DAISY: So you see, I'm not mad after all.

BOTARD: [*ironic*] Oh, Mr. Berenger says that out of chivalry— he's a very chivalrous man even if he doesn't look it.

DUDARD: What's chivalrous about saying you've seen a rhinoceros?

BOTARD: A lot—when it's said to bolster up a fantastic statement by Miss Daisy. Everybody is chivalrous to Miss Daisy, it's very understandable.

PAPILLON: Don't twist the facts, Mr. Botard. Mr. Berenger took no part in the argument. He's only just arrived.

BERENGER: [*to* DAISY] But you did see it, didn't you? We both did.

BOTARD: Pfff! It's possible that Mr. Berenger thought he saw a rhinoceros. [*He makes a sign behind* BERENGER's *back to indicate he drinks.*] He's got such a vivid imagination! Anything's possible with him!

BERENGER: I wasn't alone when I saw the rhinoceros! Or perhaps there were two rhinoceroses.

BOTARD: He doesn't even know how many he saw.

BERENGER: I was with my friend Jean! And other people were there, too.

BOTARD: [*to* BERENGER] I don't think you know what you're talking about.

DAISY: It was a unicorned rhinoceros.

BOTARD: Pff! They're in league, the two of them, to have us on.

DUDARD: [*to* DAISY] I rather think it had two horns, from what I've heard!

BOTARD: You'd better make up your minds.

PAPILLON: [*looking at the time*] That will do, gentlemen, time's getting on.

BOTARD: Did you see one rhinoceros, Mr. Berenger, or two rhinoceroses?

BERENGER: Well, it's hard to say!

BOTARD: You don't know. Miss Daisy saw one unicorned rhinoceros. What about your rhinoceros, Mr. Berenger, if indeed there was one, did it have one horn or two?

BERENGER: Exactly, that's the whole problem.

BOTARD: And it's all very dubious.

DAISY: Oh!

BOTARD: I don't mean to be offensive. But I don't believe a word of it. No rhinoceros has ever been seen in this country!

DAISY: There's a first time for everything.

BOTARD: It has never been seen! Except in school-book illustrations. Your rhinoceroses are a flower of some washerwoman's imagination.

BERENGER: The word 'flower' applied to a rhinoceros seems a bit out of place.

DUDARD: Very true.

BOTARD: [*continuing*] Your rhinoceros is a myth!

DAISY: A myth?

PAPILLON: Gentlemen I think it is high time we started to work.

BOTARD: [*to* DAISY] A myth—like flying saucers.

DUDARD: But nevertheless a cat was trampled to death—that you can't deny.

BERENGER: I was a witness to that.

DUDARD: [*pointing to* BERENGER] In front of witnesses.

BOTARD: Yes, and what a witness!

PAPILLON: Gentlemen, gentlemen!

BOTARD: [*to* DUDARD] An example of collective psychosis, Mr. Dudard. Just like religion—the opiate of the people!

DAISY: Well I believe flying saucers exist!

BOTARD: Pfff!

PAPILLON: [*firmly*] That's quite enough. There's been enough gossip! Rhinoceros or no rhinoceros, saucers or no saucers, work must go on! You're not paid to waste your time arguing about real or imaginary animals.

BOTARD: Imaginary!

DUDARD: Real!

DAISY: Very real!

PAPILLON: Gentlemen, I remind you once again that we are in working hours. I am putting an end to this futile discussion.

BOTARD: [*wounded and ironic*] Very well, Mr. Papillon. You are the Chief. Your wishes are our commands.

PAPILLON: Get on, gentlemen. I don't want to be forced to make a deduction from your salaries! Mr. Dudard, how is your report on the alcoholic repression law coming along?

DUDARD: I'm just finishing it off, sir.

PAPILLON: Then do so. It's very urgent. Mr. Berenger and Mr. Botard, have you finished correcting the proofs for the wine trade control regulations?

BERENGER: Not yet, Mr. Papillon. But they're well on the way.

PAPILLON: Then finish off the corrections together. The printers are waiting. And Miss Daisy, you bring the letters to my office for signature. Hurry up and get them typed.

DAISY: Very good, Mr. Papillon.

[DAISY *goes and types at her little desk.* DUDARD *sits at his desk and starts to work.* BERENGER *and* BOTARD *sit at their little tables in profile to the auditorium.* BOTARD, *his back to the staircase, seems in a bad temper.* BERENGER *is passive and limp; he spreads the proofs on the table, passes the manuscript to* BOTARD; BOTARD *sits down grumbling, whilst* PAPILLON *exits banging the door loudly.*]

PAPILLON: I shall see you shortly, gentlemen. [*Goes out.*]

BERENGER: [*reading and correcting whilst* BOTARD *checks the manuscript with a pencil*] Laws relating to the control of proprietary wine produce . . . [*He corrects.*] control with one L . . . [*He corrects.*] proprietary . . . one P, proprietary . . . The controlled wines of the Bordeaux region, the lower sections of the upper slopes . . .

BOTARD: I haven't got that! You've skipped a line.

BERENGER: I'll start again. The Wine Control!

DUDARD: [*to* BERENGER *and* BOTARD] Please don't read so loud. I can't concentrate with you shouting at the tops of your voices.

BOTARD: [*to* DUDARD, *over* BERENGER'S *head, resuming the recent discussion, whilst* BERENGER *continues the corrections on his own for a few moments; he moves his lips noiselessly as he reads*] It's all a hoax.

DUDARD: What's all a hoax?

BOTARD: Your rhinoceros business, of course. You've been making all this propaganda to get these rumours started!

DUDARD: [*interrupting his work*] What propaganda?

BERENGER: [*breaking in*] No question of any propaganda.

DAISY: [*interrupting her typing*] Do I have to tell you again, I saw it . . . I actually saw it, and others did, too.

DUDARD: [*to* BOTARD] You make me laugh! Propaganda! Propaganda for what?

BOTARD: [*to* DUDARD] Oh you know more about that than I do. Don't make out you're so innocent.

DUDARD: [*getting angry*] At any rate, Mr. Botard, I'm not in the pay of any furtive underground organization.

BOTARD: That's an insult, I'm not standing for that . . . [*Rises*]

BERENGER: [*pleading*] Now, now, Mr. Botard . . .

DAISY: [*to* DUDARD, *who has also risen*] Now, now, Mr. Dudard . . .

BOTARD: I tell you it's an insult.

[MR. PAPILLON'S *door suddenly opens.*] BOTARD *and* DUDARD *sit down again quickly;* MR. PAPILLON *is holding the time sheet in his hand; there is silence at his appearance.*]

PAPILLON: Is Mr. Boeuf not in today?

BERENGER: [*looking around*] No, he isn't. He must be absent.

PAPILLON: Just when I needed him. [*To* DAISY:] Did he let anyone know he was ill or couldn't come in?

DAISY: He didn't say anything to me.

PAPILLON: [*opening his door wide, and coming in*] If this goes on I shall fire him. It's not the first time he's played me this trick. Up to now I haven't said anything, but it's not going on like this. Has anyone got the key to his desk?

> [*At this moment* MRS. BOEUF *enters. She has been seen during the last speech coming up the stairs. She bursts through the door, out of breath, apprehensive.*]

BERENGER: Oh here's Mrs. Boeuf.

DAISY: Morning, Mrs. Boeuf.

MRS. BOEUF: Morning, Mr. Papillon. Good morning everyone.

PAPILLON: Well, where's your husband? What's happened to him? Is it too much trouble for him to come any more?

MRS. BOEUF: [*breathless*] Please excuse him, my husband I mean . . . he went to visit his family for the week-end. He's got a touch of flu.

PAPILLON: So he's got a touch of flu, has he?

MRS. BOEUF: [*handing a paper to* PAPILLON] He says so in the telegram. He hopes to be back on Wednesday . . . [*Almost fainting.*] Could I have a glass of water . . . and sit down a moment . . .

> [BERENGER *takes his own chair centre-stage, on which she flops.*]

PAPILLON: [*to* DAISY] Give her a glass of water.

DAISY: Yes, straightaway! [*She goes to get her a glass of water, and gives it to her during the following speeches.*]

DUDARD: [*to* PAPILLON] She must have a weak heart.

PAPILLON: It's a great nuisance that Mr. Boeuf can't come. But that's no reason for you to go to pieces.

MRS. BOEUF: [*with difficulty*] It's not . . . it's . . . well I was chased here all the way from the house by a rhinoceros . . .

BERENGER: How many horns did it have?

BOTARD: [*guffawing*] Don't make me laugh!

DUDARD: [*indignant*] Give her a chance to speak!

MRS. BOEUF: [*making a great effort to be exact, and pointing in the direction of the staircase*] It's down there, by the entrance. It seemed to want to come upstairs.

[*At this moment a noise is heard. The staircase steps are seen to crumble under an obviously formidable weight. From below an anguished trumpeting is heard. As the dust clears after the collapse of the staircase, the staircase landing is seen to be hanging in space.*]

DAISY: My God!

MRS. BOEUF: [*seated, her hand on her heart*] Oh! Ah!

[BERENGER *runs to administer to* MRS. BOEUF, *patting her cheeks and making her drink.*]

BERENGER: Keep calm!

[*Meanwhile* PAPILLON, DUDARD *and* BOTARD *rush left, jostling each other in their efforts to open the door, and stand covered in dust on the landing; the trumpetings continue to be heard.*]

DAISY: [*to* MRS. BOEUF] Are you feeling better now, Mrs. Boeuf?

PAPILLON: [*on the landing*] There it is! Down there! It is one!

BOTARD: I can't see a thing. It's an illusion.

DUDARD: Of course it's one, down there, turning round and round.

DUDARD: It can't get up here. There's no staircase any longer.

BOTARD: It's most strange. What can it mean?

DUDARD: [*turning towards* BERENGER] Come and look. Come and have a look at your rhinoceros.

BERENGER: I'm coming.

[BERENGER *rushes to the landing, followed by* DAISY *who abandons* MRS. BOEUF.]

PAPILLON: [*to* BERENGER] You're the rhinoceros expert—take a good look.

BERENGER: I'm no rhinoceros expert . . .

DAISY: Oh look at the way it's going round and round. It looks as if it was in pain . . . what can it want?

DUDARD: It seems to be looking for someone. [*To* BOTARD:] Can you see it now?

BOTARD: [*vexed*] Yes, yes, I can see it.

DAISY: [*to* PAPILLON] Perhaps we're all seeing things. You as well ...

BOTARD: I never see things. Something is definitely down there.

DUDARD: [*to* BOTARD] What do you mean, something?

PAPILLON: [*to* BERENGER] It's obviously a rhinoceros. That's what you saw before, isn't it? [*To* DAISY:] And you, too?

DAISY: Definitely.

BERENGER: It's got two horns. It's an African rhinoceros, or Asiatic rather. Oh! I don't know whether the African rhinoceros has one horn or two.

PAPILLON: It's demolished the staircase—and a good thing, too! When you think how long I've been asking the management to install stone steps in place of that worm-eaten old staircase.

DUDARD: I sent a report a week ago, Chief.

PAPILLON: It was bound to happen, I knew that. I could see it coming, and I was right.

DAISY: [*to* PAPILLON, *ironically*] As always.

BERENGER: [*to* DUDARD *and* PAPILLON] Now look, are two horns a characteristic of the Asiatic rhinoceros or the African? And is one horn a characteristic of the African or the Asiatic one ... ?

DAISY: Poor thing, it keeps on trumpeting and going round and round. What does it want? Oh, it's looking at us! [*To the rhinoceros.*] Puss, puss, puss ...

DUDARD: I shouldn't try to stroke it, it's probably not tame ...

PAPILLON: In any case, it's out of reach.

[*The rhinoceros gives a horrible trumpeting.*]

DAISY: Poor thing!

BERENGER: [*to* BOTARD, *still insisting*] You're very well informed, don't you think that the ones with two horns are ...

PAPILLON: What are you rambling on about, Berenger? You're still a bit under the weather, Mr. Botard was right.

BOTARD: How can it be possible in a civilized country ... ?

DAISY: [*to* BOTARD] All right. But does it exist or not?

BOTARD: It's all an infamous plot! [*With a political orator's gesture he points to* DUDARD, *quelling him with a look.*] It's all your fault!

DUDARD: Why mine, rather than yours?

BOTARD: [*furious*] Mine? It's always the little people who get the blame. If I had my way . . .

PAPILLON: We're in a fine mess with no staircase.

DAISY: [*to* BOTARD *and* DUDARD] Calm down, this is no time to quarrel!

PAPILLON: It's all the management's fault.

DAISY: Maybe. But how are we going to get down?

PAPILLON: [*joking amorously and caressing* DAISY's *cheek*] I'll take you in my arms and we'll float down together.

DAISY: [*rejecting* PAPILLON's *advances*] You keep your horny hands off my face, you old pachyderm!

PAPILLON: I was only joking!

[*Meanwhile the rhinoceros has continued its trumpeting.* MRS. BOEUF *has risen and joined the group. For a few moments she stares fixedly at the rhinoceros turning round and round below; suddenly she lets out a terrible cry.*]

MRS. BOEUF: My God! It can't be true!

BERENGER: [*to* MRS. BOEUF] What's the matter?

MRS. BOEUF: It's my husband. Oh Boeuf, my poor Boeuf, what's happened to you?

DAISY: [*to* MRS. BOEUF] Are you positive?

MRS. BOEUF: I recognize him, I recognize him!

[*The rhinoceros replies with a violent but tender trumpeting.*]

PAPILLON: Well! That's the last straw. This time he's fired for good!

DUDARD: Is he insured?

BOTARD: [*aside*] I understand it all now . . .

DAISY: How can you collect insurance in a case like this?

MRS. BOEUF: [*fainting into* BERENGER's *arms*] Oh! My God!

BERENGER: Oh!

DAISY: Carry her over here!

[BERENGER, *helped by* DUDARD *and* DAISY, *installs* MRS. BOEUF *in a chair.*]

DUDARD: [*while they are carrying her*] Don't upset yourself, Mrs. Boeuf.

MRS. BOEUF: Ah! Oh!

DAISY: Maybe it can all be put right . . .

PAPILLON: [*to* DUDARD] Legally, what can be done?

DUDARD: You need to get a solicitor's advice.

BOTARD: [*following the procession, raising his hands to heaven*] It's the sheerest madness! What a society!

> [*They crowd round* MRS. BOEUF, *pinching her cheeks; she opens her eyes, emits an 'Ah' and closes them again; they continue to pinch her cheeks as* BOTARD *speaks:*]

You can be certain of one thing: I shall report this to my union. I don't desert a colleague in the hour of need. It won't be hushed up.

MRS. BOEUF: [*coming to*] My poor darling, I can't leave him like that, my poor darling. [*A trumpeting is heard.*] He's calling me. [*Tenderly*] He's calling me.

DAISY: Feeling better now, Mrs. Boeuf?

DUDARD: She's picking up a bit.

BOTARD: [*to* MRS. BOEUF] You can count on the union's support. Would you like to become a member of the committee?

PAPILLON: Work's going to be delayed again. What about the post, Miss Daisy?

DAISY: I want to know first how we're going to get out of here.

PAPILLON: It is a problem. Through the window.

> [*They all go to the window with the exception of* MRS. BOEUF *slumped in her chair and* BOTARD *who stays centre-stage.*]

BOTARD: I know where it came from.

DAISY: [*at window*] It's too high.

BERENGER: Perhaps we ought to call the firemen, and get them to bring ladders!

PAPILLON: Miss Daisy, go to my office and telephone the fire brigade. [*He makes as if to follow her.*]

> [DAISY *goes out up-stage and one hears her voice on the telephone say: 'Hello, hello, is that the Fire Brigade?' followed by a vague sound of telephone conversation.*]

MRS. BOEUF: [*rising suddenly*] I can't desert him, I can't desert him now!

PAPILLON: If you want to divorce him . . . you'd be perfectly justified.

DUDARD: You'd be the injured party.

MRS. BOEUF: No! Poor thing! This is not the moment for that. I won't abandon my husband in such a state.

BOTARD: You're a good woman.

DUDARD: [to MRS. BOEUF] But what are you going to do?

[She runs left towards the landing.]

BERENGER: Watch out!

MRS. BOEUF: I can't leave him, I can't leave him now!

DUDARD: Hold her back!

MRS. BOEUF: I'm taking him home!

PAPILLON: What's she trying to do?

MRS. BOEUF: [preparing to jump; on the edge of the landing] I'm coming my darling, I'm coming!

BERENGER: She's going to jump.

BOTARD: It's no more than her duty.

DUDARD: She can't do that.

[Everyone with the exception of DAISY, who is still telephoning, is near to MRS. BOEUF on the landing; she jumps; BERENGER who tries to restrain her, is left with her skirt in his hand.]

BERENGER: I couldn't hold her back.

[The rhinoceros is heard from below, tenderly trumpeting.]

VOICE OF MRS. BOEUF: Here I am, my sweet, I'm here now.

DUDARD: She landed on his back in the saddle.

BOTARD: She's a good rider.

VOICE OF MRS. BOEUF: Home now, dear, let's go home.

DUDARD: They're off at a gallop.

[DUDARD, BOTARD, BERENGER, PAPILLON come back on-stage and go to the window.]

BERENGER: They're moving fast.

DUDARD: [to PAPILLON] Ever done any riding?

PAPILLON: A bit . . . a long time ago . . . [Turning to the up-stage door, to DUDARD:] Is she still on the telephone?

BERENGER: [following the course of the rhinoceros] They're already a long way off. They're out of sight.

DAISY: [*coming on-stage*] I had trouble getting the firemen.

BOTARD: [*as if concluding an interior monologue*] A fine state of affairs!

DAISY: . . . I had trouble getting the firemen!

PAPILLON: Are there fires all over the place, then?

BERENGER: I agree with Mr. Botard. Mrs. Boeuf's attitude is very moving; she's a woman of feeling.

PAPILLON: It means one employee less, who has to be replaced.

BERENGER: Do you really think he's no use to us any more?

DAISY: No, there aren't any fires, the firemen have been called out for other rhinoceroses.

BERENGER: For other rhinoceroses?

DAISY: Yes, other rhinoceroses. They've been reported all over the town. This morning there were seven, now there are seventeen.

BOTARD: What did I tell you?

DAISY: As many as thirty-two have been reported. They're not official yet, but they're bound to be confirmed soon.

BOTARD: [*less certain*] Pff!! They always exaggerate.

PAPILLON: Are they coming to get us out of here?

BERENGER: I'm hungry . . . !

DAISY: Yes, they're coming; the firemen are on the way.

PAPILLON: What about the work?

DUDARD: It looks as if it's out of our hands.

PAPILLON: We'll have to make up the lost time.

DUDARD: Well, Mr. Botard, do you still deny all rhinocerotic evidence?

BOTARD: Our union is against your dismissing Mr. Boeuf without notice.

PAPILLON: It's not up to me; we shall see what conclusions they reach at the enquiry.

BOTARD: [*to* DUDARD] No, Mr. Dudard, I do not deny the rhinocerotic evidence. I never have.

DUDARD: That's not true.

DAISY: Oh no, that's not true.

BOTARD: I repeat I have never denied it. I just wanted to find

out exactly where it was all leading. Because I know my own
mind. I'm not content to simply state that a phenomenon
exists. I make it my business to understand and explain it. At
least I could explain it if . . .

DUDARD: Then explain it to us.

DAISY: Yes, explain it, Mr. Botard.

PAPILLON: Explain it, when your colleagues ask you.

BOTARD: I will explain it . . .

DUDARD: We're all listening.

DAISY: I'm most curious.

BOTARD: I will explain it . . . one day . . .

DUDARD: Why not now?

BOTARD: [menacingly; to MR. PAPILLON] We'll go into the
explanation later, in private. [To everyone:] I know the whys
and the wherefores of this whole business . . .

DAISY: What whys?

BERENGER: What wherefores?

DUDARD: I'd give a lot to know these whys and wherefores . . .

BOTARD: [continuing; with a terrible air] And I also know the
names of those responsible. The names of the traitors. You
can't fool me. I'll let you know the purpose and the meaning
of this whole plot! I'll unmask the perpetrators!

BERENGER: But who'd want to . . .

DUDARD: [to BOTARD] You're evading the question, Mr. Botard.

PAPILLON: Let's have no evasions.

BOTARD: Evading? What, me?

DAISY: Just now you accused us of suffering from hallucinations.

BOTARD: Just now, yes. Now the hallucination has become a
provocation.

DUDARD: And how do you consider this change came about?

BOTARD: It's an open secret, gentlemen. Even the man in the
street knows about it. Only hypocrites pretend not to understand.

[The noise and hooting of a fire-engine is heard. The brakes are
abruptly applied just under the window.]

DAISY: That's the firemen!

BOTARD: There're going to be some big changes made; they won't get away with it as easily as that.

DUDARD: That doesn't mean anything, Mr. Botard. The rhinoceroses exist, and that's that. That's all there is to it.

DAISY: [*at the window, looking down*] Up here, firemen!

[*A bustling is heard below, commotion, engine noises.*]

VOICE OF FIREMAN: Put up the ladder!

BOTARD: [*to* DUDARD] I hold the key to all these happenings, an infallible system of interpretation.

PAPILLON: I want you all back in the office this afternoon.

[*The firemen's ladder is placed against the window.*]

BOTARD: Too bad about the office, Mr. Papillon.

PAPILLON: I don't know what the management will say!

DUDARD: These are exceptional circumstances.

BOTARD: [*pointing to the window*] They can't force us to come back this way. We'll have to wait till the staircase is repaired.

DUDARD: If anyone breaks a leg, it'll be the management's responsibility.

PAPILLON: That's true.

[*A fireman's helmet is seen, followed by the fireman.*]

BERENGER: [*to* DAISY *pointing to the window*] After you, Miss Daisy.

FIREMAN: Come on, Miss.

[*The fireman takes* DAISY *in his arms; she steps astride the window and disappears with him.*]

DUDARD: Good-bye Miss Daisy. See you soon.

DAISY: [*disappearing*] See you soon, good-bye!

PAPILLON: [*at window*] Telephone me tomorrow morning, Miss Daisy. You can come and type the letters at my house. [*To* BERENGER:] Mr. Berenger, I draw your attention to the fact that we are not on holiday, and that work will resume as soon as possible. [*To the other two:*] You hear what I say, gentlemen?

DUDARD: Of course, Mr. Papillon.

BOTARD: They'll go on exploiting us till we drop, of course.

FIREMAN: [*reappearing at window*] Who's next?

PAPILLON: [*to all three of them*] Go on!

DUDARD: After you, Mr. Papillon.

BERENGER: After you, Chief.

BOTARD: You first, of course.

PAPILLON: [*to* BERENGER] Bring me Miss Daisy's letters. There, on the table.

[BERENGER *goes and gets the letters, brings them to* PAPILLON.]

FIREMAN: Come on, hurry up. We've not got all day. We've got other calls to make.

BOTARD: What did I tell you?

[PAPILLON, *the letters under his arm, steps astride the window*.]

PAPILLON: [*to the* FIREMAN] Careful of the documents! [*Turning to the others:*] Good-bye, gentlemen.

DUDARD: Good-bye, Mr. Papillon.

BERENGER: Good-bye, Mr. Papillon.

PAPILLON: [*he has disappeared; one hears him say*] Careful of my papers. Dudard! Lock up the offices!

DUDARD: [*shouting*] Don't you worry, Mr. Papillon. [*To* BOTARD:] After you, Mr. Botard.

BOTARD: I am about to descend, gentlemen. And I am going to take this matter up immediately with the proper authorities. I'll get to the bottom of this so-called mystery. [*He moves to window*.]

DUDARD: [*to* BOTARD] I thought it was all perfectly clear to you!

BOTARD: [*astride the window*] Your irony doesn't affect me. What I'm after are the proofs and the documents—yes, proof positive of your treason.

DUDARD: That's absurd . . .

BOTARD: Your insults . . .

DUDARD: [*interrupting him*] It's you who are insulting me . . .

BOTARD: [*disappearing*] I don't insult. I merely prove.

VOICE OF FIREMAN: Come on there!

DUDARD: [*to* BERENGER] What are you doing this afternoon? Shall we meet for a drink?

BERENGER: Sorry, I can't. I'm taking advantage of this afternoon off to go and see my friend Jean. I do want to make it up with him, after all. We got carried away. It was all my fault.

[*The fireman's head reappears at the window.*]

FIREMAN: Come along there!

BERENGER: [*pointing to the window*] After you.

DUDARD: After you.

BERENGER: Oh no, after you.

DUDARD: No, I insist, after you.

BERENGER: No, please, after you, after you.

FIREMAN: Hurry up!

DUDARD: After you, after you.

BERENGER: No, after you, after you.

[*They climb through the window together. The fireman helps them down, as the curtain falls.*]

CURTAIN

ACT TWO

SCENE TWO

JEAN's *house. The layout is roughly the same as Act Two, Scene One. That is to say, the stage is divided into two. To the right, occupying three-quarters or four-fifths of the stage, according to size, is* JEAN's *bedroom. Up-stage, a chair or an armchair, on which* BERENGER *will sit. Right centre, a door leading to* JEAN's *bathroom. When* JEAN *goes in to wash, the noise of a tap is heard, and that of the shower. To the left of the room, a partition divides the stage in two. Centre-stage, the door leading to the stairs. If a less realistic, more stylized décor is preferred, the door may be placed without a partition. To the left is the staircase; the top steps are visible, leading to* JEAN's *flat, the banister and the landing. At the back, on the landing level, is the door to the neighbour's flat. Lower down, at the back, there is a glass door, over which is written: 'Concierge'.*

[*When the curtain rises,* JEAN *is in bed, lying under the blanket, his back to the audience. One hears him cough.*

After a few moments BERENGER *is seen, climbing the top steps of the staircase. He knocks at the door;* JEAN *does not answer.* BERENGER *knocks again.*]

BERENGER: Jean! [*He knocks again.*] Jean!

[*The door at the end of the landing opens slightly, and a little old man with a white goatee appears.*]

OLD MAN: What is it?

BERENGER: I want to see Jean. I am a friend of his.

OLD MAN: I thought it was me you wanted. My name's Jean as well, but it's the other one you want.

VOICE OF OLD MAN'S WIFE: [*from within the room*] Is it for us?

OLD MAN: [*turning to his wife who is not seen*] No, for the other one.

BERENGER: [*knocking*] Jean!

OLD MAN: I didn't see him go out. But I saw him last night. He looked in a bad temper.

BERENGER: Yes, I know why; it was my fault.

OLD MAN: Perhaps he doesn't feel like opening the door to you. Try again.

VOICE OF OLD MAN'S WIFE: Jean, don't stand gossiping, Jean!

BERENGER: [*knocking*] Jean!

OLD MAN: [*to his wife*] Just a moment. Oh dear, dear . . . [*He closes the door and disappears.*]

JEAN: [*still lying down, his back to the audience, in a hoarse voice*] What is it?

BERENGER: I've dropped by to see you, Jean.

JEAN: Who is it?

BERENGER: It's me, Berenger. I hope I'm not disturbing you.

JEAN: Oh it's you, is it? Come in!

BERENGER: [*trying to open the door*] The door's locked.

JEAN: Just a moment. Oh dear, dear . . . [JEAN *gets up in a pretty bad temper. He is wearing green pyjamas, his hair is tousled.*] Just a moment. [*He unlocks the door.*] Just a moment. [*He goes back to bed, gets under the blanket.*] Come in!

BERENGER: [*coming in*] Hello Jean!

JEAN: [*in bed*] What time is it? Aren't you at the office?

BERENGER: You're still in bed; you're not at the office, then? Sorry if I'm disturbing you.

JEAN: [*still with his back turned*] Funny, I didn't recognize your voice.

BERENGER: I didn't recognize yours either.

JEAN: [*still with his back turned*] Sit down!

BERENGER: Aren't you feeling well?

[JEAN *replies with a grunt.*]

You know, Jean, it was stupid of me to get so upset yesterday over a thing like that.

JEAN: A thing like what?

BERENGER: Yesterday ...

JEAN: When yesterday? Where yesterday?

BERENGER: Don't you remember? It was about that wretched rhinoceros.

JEAN: What rhinoceros?

BERENGER: The rhinoceros, or rather, the two wretched rhinoceroses we saw.

JEAN: Oh yes, I remember ... How do you know they were wretched?

BERENGER: Oh I just said that.

JEAN: Oh. Well let's not talk any more about it.

BERENGER: That's very nice of you.

JEAN: Then that's that.

BERENGER: But I would like to say how sorry I am for being so insistent ... and so obstinate ... and getting so angry ... in fact ... I acted stupidly.

JEAN: That's not surprising with you.

BERENGER: I'm very sorry.

JEAN: I don't feel very well. [*He coughs.*]

BERENGER: That's probably why you're in bed. [*With a change of tone:*] You know, Jean, as it turned out, we were both right.

JEAN: What about?

BERENGER: About ... well, you know, the same thing. Sorry to bring it up again, but I'll only mention it briefly. I just wanted you to know that in our different ways we were both right.

It's been proved now. There are some rhinoceroses in the town with two horns and some with one.

JEAN: That's what I told you! Well, that's just too bad.

BERENGER: Yes, too bad.

JEAN: Or maybe it's all to the good; it depends.

BERENGER: [*continuing*] In the final analysis it doesn't much matter which comes from where. The important thing, as I see it, is the fact that they're there at all, because ...

JEAN: [*turning and sitting on his unmade bed, facing* BERENGER] I don't feel well, I don't feel well at all!

BERENGER: Oh I am sorry! What do you think it is?

JEAN: I don't know exactly, there's something wrong somewhere ...

BERENGER: Do you feel weak?

JEAN: Not at all. On the contrary, I feel full of beans.

BERENGER: I meant just a passing weakness. It happens to everybody.

JEAN: It never happens to me.

BERENGER: Perhaps you're too healthy then. Too much energy can be a bad thing. It unsettles the nervous system.

JEAN: My nervous system is in perfect order. [*His voice has become more and more hoarse.*] I'm sound in mind and limb. I come from a long line of ...

BERENGER: I know you do. Perhaps you've just caught a chill. Have you got a temperature?

JEAN: I don't know. Yes, probably I have a touch of fever. My head aches.

BERENGER: Just a slight migraine. Would you like me to leave you alone?

JEAN: No, stay. You don't worry me.

BERENGER: Your voice is hoarse, too.

JEAN: Hoarse?

BERENGER: A bit hoarse, yes. That's why I didn't recognize it.

JEAN: Why should I be hoarse? My voice hasn't changed; it's yours that's changed!

BERENGER: Mine?

JEAN: Why not?

BERENGER: It's possible. I hadn't noticed.

JEAN: I sometimes wonder if you're capable of noticing anything. [*Putting his hand to his forehead.*] Actually it's my forehead that hurts. I must have given it a knock. [*His voice is even hoarser.*]

BERENGER: When did you do that?

JEAN: I don't know. I don't remember it happening.

BERENGER: But it must have hurt you.

JEAN: I must have done it while I was asleep.

BERENGER: The shock would have wakened you up. You must have just dreamed you knocked yourself.

JEAN: I never dream . . .

BERENGER: [*continuing*] Your headache must have come on while you were asleep. You've forgotten you dreamed, or rather you only remember subconsciously.

JEAN: Subconsciously, me? I'm master of my own thoughts, my mind doesn't wander. I think straight, I always think straight.

BERENGER: I know that. I haven't made myself clear.

JEAN: Then make yourself clearer. And you needn't bother to make any of your unpleasant observations to me.

BERENGER: One often has the impression that one has knocked oneself when one has a headache. [*Coming closer to* JEAN.] If you'd really knocked yourself, you'd have a bump. [*Looking at* JEAN.] Oh, you've got one, you do have a bump, in fact.

JEAN: A bump?

BERENGER: Just a tiny one.

JEAN: Where?

BERENGER: [*pointing to* JEAN's *forehead*] There, it starts just above your nose.

JEAN: I've no bump. We've never had bumps in my family.

BERENGER: Have you got a mirror?

JEAN: That's the limit! [*Touching his forehead.*] I can feel something. I'm going to have a look, in the bathroom. [*He gets up abruptly and goes to the bathroom.* BERENGER *watches him as he goes. Then, from the bathroom:*] It's true, I have got a bump. [*He comes back; his skin has become greener.*] So you see I did knock myself.

BERENGER: You don't look well, your skin is quite green.

JEAN: You seem to delight in saying disagreeable things to me. Have you taken a look at yourself lately?

BERENGER: Forgive me. I didn't mean to upset you.

JEAN: [*very hoarse*] That's hard to believe.

BERENGER: Your breathing's very heavy. Does your throat hurt?
    [JEAN *goes and sits on his bed again.*]
    If your throat hurts, perhaps it's a touch of quinsy.

JEAN: Why should I have a touch of quinsy?

BERENGER: It's nothing to be ashamed of—I sometimes get it. Let me feel your pulse. [*He rises and takes* JEAN's *pulse.*]

JEAN: [*in an even hoarser voice*] Oh, it'll pass.

BERENGER: Your pulse is normal. You needn't get alarmed.

JEAN: I'm not alarmed in the slightest—why should I be?

BERENGER: You're right. A few days' rest will put you right.

JEAN: I've no time to rest. I must go and buy some food.

BERENGER: There's not much the matter with you, if you're hungry. But even so, you ought to take a few days' rest. It's wise to take care. Has the doctor been to see you?

JEAN: I don't need a doctor.

BERENGER: Oh but you ought to get the doctor.

JEAN: You're not going to get the doctor because I don't want the doctor. I can look after myself.

BERENGER: You shouldn't reject medical advice.

JEAN: Doctors invent illnesses that don't exist.

BERENGER: They do it in good faith—just for the pleasure of looking after people.

JEAN: They invent illnesses, they invent them, I tell you.

BERENGER: Perhaps they do—but after they invent them they cure them.

JEAN: I only have confidence in veterinary surgeons. There!

BERENGER: [*who has released* JEAN's *wrist, now takes it up again*] Your veins look swollen. They're jutting out.

JEAN: It's a sign of virility.

BERENGER: Of course it's a sign of health and strength. But ...
[*He examines* JEAN'S *forearm more closely, until* JEAN *violently withdraws it.*]

JEAN: What do you think you're doing—scrutinizing me as if I were some strange animal?

BERENGER: It's your skin ...

JEAN: What's my skin got to do with you? I don't go on about your skin, do I?

BERENGER: It's just that ... it seems to be changing colour all the time. It's going green. [*He tries to take* JEAN'S *hand.*] It's hardening as well.

JEAN: [*withdrawing his hand again*] Stop mauling me about! What's the matter with you? You're getting on my nerves.

BERENGER: [*to himself*] Perhaps it's more serious than I thought. [*To* JEAN:] We must get the doctor. [*He goes to the telephone.*]

JEAN: Leave that thing alone. [*He darts over to* BERENGER *and pushes him.* BERENGER *staggers.*] You mind your own business.

BERENGER: All right. It was for your own good.

JEAN: [*coughing and breathing noisily*] I know better than you what's good for me.

BERENGER: You're breathing very hard.

JEAN: One breathes as best one can. You don't like the way I breathe, and I don't like the way you breathe. Your breathing's too feeble, you can't even hear it; it's as if you were going to drop dead any moment.

BERENGER: I know I'm not as strong as you.

JEAN: I don't keep trying to get you to the doctor, do I? Leave people to do as they please.

BERENGER: Don't get angry with me. You know very well I'm your friend.

JEAN: There's no such thing as friendship. I don't believe in your friendship.

BERENGER: That's a very hurtful thing to say.

JEAN: There's nothing for you to get hurt about.

BERENGER: My dear Jean ...

JEAN: I'm not your dear Jean.

BERENGER: You're certainly in a very misanthropic mood today.

JEAN: Yes, I am misanthropic, very misanthropic indeed. I like being misanthropic.

BERENGER: You're probably still angry with me over our silly quarrel yesterday. I admit it was my fault. That's why I came to say I was sorry . . .

JEAN: What quarrel are you talking about?

BERENGER: I told you just now. You know, about the rhinoceros.

JEAN: [*not listening to* BERENGER] It's not that I hate people. I'm just indifferent to them—or rather, they disgust me; and they'd better keep out of my way, or I'll run them down.

BERENGER: You know very well that I shall never stand in your way.

JEAN: I've got one aim in life. And I'm making straight for it.

BERENGER: I'm sure you're right. But I feel you're passing through a moral crisis.

> [JEAN *has been pacing the room like a wild beast in a cage, from one wall to the other.* BERENGER *watches him, occasionally stepping aside to avoid him.* JEAN's *voice has become more and more hoarse.*]

You mustn't excite yourself, it's bad for you.

JEAN: I felt uncomfortable in my clothes; now my pyjamas irritate me as well. [*He undoes his pyjama jacket and does it up again.*]

BERENGER: But whatever's the matter with your skin?

JEAN: Can't you leave my skin alone? I certainly wouldn't want to change it for yours.

BERENGER: It's gone like leather.

JEAN: That makes it more solid. It's weatherproof.

BERENGER: You're getting greener and greener.

JEAN: You've got colour mania today. You're seeing things, you've been drinking again.

BERENGER: I did yesterday, but not today.

JEAN: It's the result of all your past debauches.

BERENGER: I promised you to turn over a new leaf. I take notice when friends like you give me advice. And I never feel humiliated—on the contrary!

JEAN: I don't care what you feel. Brrr . . .

BERENGER: What did you say?

JEAN: I didn't say anything. I just went Brrrr ... because I felt like it.

BERENGER: [*looking fixedly at* JEAN] Do you know what's happened to Boeuf? He's turned into a rhinoceros.

JEAN: What happened to Boeuf?

BERENGER: He's turned into a rhinoceros.

JEAN: [*fanning himself with the flaps of his jacket*] Brrr ...

BERENGER: Come on now, stop joking.

JEAN: I can puff if I want to, can't I? I've every right ... I'm in my own house.

BERENGER: I didn't say you couldn't.

JEAN: And I shouldn't if I were you. I feel hot, I feel hot. Brrr ... Just a moment. I must cool myself down.

BERENGER: [*whilst* JEAN *darts to the bathroom*] He must have a fever. [JEAN *is in the bathroom, one hears him puffing, and also the sound of a running tap.*]

JEAN: [*off*] Brrr ...

BERENGER: He's got the shivers. I'm jolly well going to 'phone the doctor. [*He goes to the telephone again then comes back quickly when he hears* JEAN's *voice.*]

JEAN: [*off*] So old Boeuf turned into a rhinoceros, did he? Ah, ah, ah ... ! He was just having you on, he'd disguised himself. [*He pokes his head round the bathroom door. He is very green. The bump over his nose is slightly larger.*] He was just disguised.

BERENGER: [*walking about the room, without seeing* JEAN] He looked very serious about it, I assure you.

JEAN: Oh well, that's his business.

BERENGER: [*turning to* JEAN *who disappears again into the bathroom*] I'm sure he didn't do it on purpose. He didn't want to change.

JEAN: [*off*] How do you know?

BERENGER: Well, everything led one to suppose so.

JEAN: And what if he did do it on purpose? Eh? What if he did it on purpose?

BERENGER: I'd be very surprised. At any rate, Mrs. Boeuf didn't seem to know about it ...

JEAN: [*in a very hoarse voice*] Ah, ah, ah! Fat old Mrs. Boeuf. She's just a fool!

BERENGER: Well fool or no fool . . .

JEAN: [*he enters swiftly, takes off his jacket, and throws it on the bed. BERENGER discreetly averts his gaze. JEAN, whose back and chest are now green, goes back into the bathroom. As he walks in and out:*] Boeuf never let his wife know what he was up to . . .

BERENGER: You're wrong there, Jean—it was a very united family.

JEAN: Very united, was it? Are you sure? Hum, hum, Brr . . .

BERENGER: [*moving to the bathroom, where JEAN slams the door in his face*] Very united. And the proof is that . . .

JEAN: [*from within*] Boeuf led his own private life. He had a secret side to him deep down which he kept to himself.

BERENGER: I shouldn't make you talk, it seems to upset you.

JEAN: On the contrary, it relaxes me.

BERENGER: Even so, let me call the doctor, I beg you.

JEAN: I absolutely forbid it. I can't stand obstinate people.

[*JEAN comes back into the bedroom. BERENGER backs away a little scared, for JEAN is greener than ever and speaks only with difficulty. His voice is unrecognizable.*]

Well, whether he changes into a rhinoceros on purpose or against his will, he's probably all the better for it.

BERENGER: How can you say a thing like that? Surely you don't think . . .

JEAN: You always see the black side of everything. It obviously gave him great pleasure to turn into a rhinoceros. There's nothing extraordinary in that.

BERENGER: There's nothing extraordinary in it, but I doubt if it gave him much pleasure.

JEAN: And why not, pray?

BERENGER: It's hard to say exactly why; it's just something you feel.

JEAN: I tell you it's not as bad as all that. After all, rhinoceroses are living creatures the same as us; they've got as much right to life as we have!

BERENGER: As long as they don't destroy ours in the process. You must admit the difference in mentality.

JEAN: [*pacing up and down the room, and in and out of the bathroom*] Are you under the impression that our way of life is superior?

BERENGER: Well at any rate, we have our own moral standards which I consider incompatible with the standards of these animals.

JEAN: Moral standards! I'm sick of moral standards! We need to go beyond moral standards!

BERENGER: What would you put in their place?

JEAN: [*still pacing*] Nature!

BERENGER: Nature?

JEAN: Nature has its own laws. Morality's against Nature.

BERENGER: Are you suggesting we replace our moral laws by the law of the jungle?

JEAN: It would suit me, suit me fine.

BERENGER: You say that. But deep down, no one . . .

JEAN: [*interrupting him, pacing up and down*] We've got to build our life on new foundations. We must get back to primeval integrity.

BERENGER: I don't agree with you at all.

JEAN: [*breathing noisily*] I can't breathe.

BERENGER: Just think a moment. You must admit that we have a philosophy that animals don't share, and an irreplaceable set of values, which it's taken centuries of human civilization to build up . . .

JEAN: [*in the bathroom*] When we've demolished all that, we'll be better off!

BERENGER: I know you don't mean that seriously. You're joking! It's just a poetic fancy.

JEAN: Brrr. [*He almost trumpets.*]

BERENGER: I'd never realized you were a poet.

JEAN: [*comes out of the bathroom*] Brrr. [*He trumpets again.*]

BERENGER: That's not what you believe fundamentally—I know you too well. You know as well as I do that mankind . . .

JEAN: [*interrupting him*] Don't talk to me about mankind!

BERENGER: I mean the human individual, humanism . . .

JEAN: Humanism is all washed up! You're a ridiculous old sentimentalist. [*He goes into the bathroom.*]

BERENGER: But you must admit that the mind . . .

JEAN: [*from the bathroom*] Just clichés! You're talking rubbish!

BERENGER: Rubbish!

JEAN: [*from the bathroom in a very hoarse voice, difficult to understand*] Utter rubbish!

BERENGER: I'm amazed to hear you say that, Jean, really! You must be out of your mind. You wouldn't like to be a rhinoceros yourself, now would you?

JEAN: Why not? I'm not a victim of prejudice like you.

BERENGER: Can you speak more clearly? I didn't catch what you said. You swallowed the words.

JEAN: [*still in the bathroom*] Then keep your ears open.

BERENGER: What?

JEAN: Keep your ears open. I said what's wrong with being a rhinoceros? I'm all for change.

BERENGER: It's not like you to say a thing like that . . .

[BERENGER *stops short, for* JEAN'S *appearance is truly alarming.* JEAN *has become, in fact, completely green. The bump on his forehead is practically a rhinoceros horn.*]

Oh! You really must be out of your mind!

[JEAN *dashes to his bed, throws the covers on the floor, talking in a fast and furious gabble, and making very weird sounds.*]

You mustn't get into such a state—calm down! I hardly recognize you any more.

JEAN: [*hardly distinguishable*] Hot . . . far too hot! Demolish the lot, clothes itch, they itch! [*He drops his pyjama trousers.*]

BERENGER: What are you doing? You're not yourself! You're generally so modest!

JEAN: The swamps! The swamps!

BERENGER: Look at me! Can't you see me any longer? Can't you hear me?

JEAN: I can hear you perfectly well! I can see you perfectly well!

[*He lunges towards* BERENGER, *head down.* BERENGER *gets out of the way.*]

BERENGER: Watch out!

JEAN: [*puffing noisily*] Sorry! [*He darts at great speed into the bath·room.*]

BERENGER: [*makes as if to escape by the door left, then comes back and goes into the bathroom after* JEAN, *saying*] I really can't leave him like that—after all he is a friend. [*From the bathroom:*] I'm going to get the doctor! It's absolutely necessary, believe me!

JEAN: [*from the bathroom*] No!

BERENGER: [*from the bathroom*] Calm down, Jean, you're being ridiculous! Oh, your horn's getting longer and longer—you're a rhinoceros!

JEAN: [*from the bathroom*] I'll trample you, I'll trample you down! [*A lot of noise comes from the bathroom, trumpetings, objects falling, the sound of a shattered mirror; then* BERENGER *reappears, very frightened; he closes the bathroom door with difficulty against the resistance that is being made from inside.*]

BERENGER: [*pushing against the door*] He's a rhinoceros, he's a rhinoceros!

[BERENGER *manages to close the door. As he does so, his coat is pierced by a rhinoceros horn. The door shakes under the animal's constant pressure and the din continues in the bathroom; trumpetings are heard, interspersed with indistinct phrases such as:* 'I'm furious! The swine!' *etc.* BERENGER *rushes to the door right.*] I never would have thought it of him—never! [*He opens the staircase door and goes and knocks at the landing door; he bangs repeatedly on it with his fist.*] There's a rhinoceros in the building! Get the police!

OLD MAN: [*poking his head out*] What's the matter?

BERENGER: Get the police! There's a rhinoceros in the house!

VOICE OF OLD MAN'S WIFE: What are you up to, Jean? Why are you making all that noise?

OLD MAN: [*to his wife*] I don't know what he's talking about. He's seen a rhinoceros.

BERENGER: Yes, here in the house. Get the police!

OLD MAN: What do you think you're up to, disturbing people like that. What a way to behave! [*He shuts the door in his face.*]

BERENGER: [*rushing to the stairs*] Porter, porter, there's a rhinoceros in the house, get the police! Porter!

[*The upper part of the porter's lodge is seen to open; the head of a rhinoceros appears.*]

Another!

[BERENGER *rushes upstairs again. He wants to go back into* JEAN'S *room, hesitates, then makes for the door of the* OLD MAN *again. At this moment the door of the room opens to reveal two rhinoceros heads.*]

Oh, my God!

[BERENGER *goes back into* JEAN'S *room where the bathroom door is still shaking. He goes to the window which is represented simply by the frame, facing the audience. He is exhausted, almost fainting; he murmurs.*]

My God! Oh my God!

[*He makes a gigantic effort, and manages to get astride the window (that is, towards the audience) but gets back again quickly, for at the same time, crossing the orchestra pit at great speed, move a large number of rhinoceros heads in line.* BERENGER *gets back with all speed, looks out of the window for a moment.*]

There's a whole herd of them in the street now! An army of rhinoceroses, surging up the avenue . . . ! [*He looks all around.*] Where can I get out? Where can I get out? If only they'd keep to the middle of the road! They're all over the pavement as well. Where can I get out? Where can I get out?

[*Distracted, he goes from door to door and to the window, whilst the bathroom door continues to shake and* JEAN *continues to trumpet and hurl incomprehensible insults. This continues for some moments; whenever* BERENGER *in his disordered attempts to escape reaches the door of the Old People's flat or the stairway, he is greeted by rhinoceros heads which trumpet and cause him to beat a hasty retreat. He goes to the window for the last time and looks out.*]

A whole herd of them! And they always said the rhinoceros

was a solitary animal! That's not true, that's a conception they'll have to revise! They've smashed up all the public benches. [*He wrings his hands.*] What's to be done?

[*He goes once more to the various exits, but the spectacle of the rhinoceros halts him. When he gets back to the bathroom door it seems about to give way.* BERENGER *throws himself against the back wall, which yields; the street is visible in the background; he flees, shouting:*]

Rhinoceros! Rhinoceros!

[*Noises. The bathroom door is on the point of yielding.*]

CURTAIN

ACT THREE

The arrangement is roughly the same as in the previous scene.

It is BERENGER'S *room, which bears a striking resemblance to that of* JEAN.   *Only certain details, one or two extra pieces of furniture, reveal that it is a different room. Staircase to the left, and landing. Door at the end of the landing. There is no porter's lodge. Up-stage is a divan.*

An armchair, and a little table with a telephone. Perhaps an extra telephone, and a chair. Window up-stage, open. A window frame in the foreground.

BERENGER *is lying on his divan, his back to the audience.* BERENGER *is lying fully dressed. His head is bandaged. He seems to be having a bad dream, and writhes in his sleep.*

BERENGER: No. [*Pause*] Watch out for the horns! [*Pause*]

[*The noise of a considerable number of rhinoceroses is heard passing under the up-stage window.*]

No! [*He falls to the floor still fighting with what he has seen in his dream, and wakes up. He puts his hand to his head with an apprehensive air, then moves to the mirror and lifts his bandage, as the noises fade away. He heaves a sigh of relief when he sees he has no bump.*

*He hesitates, goes to the divan, lies down, and instantly gets up
again. He goes to the table where he takes up a bottle of brandy and a
glass, and is about to pour himself a drink. Then after a short
internal struggle he replaces the bottle and glass.]* Now, now,
where's your will-power! *[He wants to go back to his divan, but
the rhinoceroses are heard again under the up-stage window. The
noises stop; he goes to the little table, hesitates a moment, then with
a gesture of 'Oh what's it matter!' he pours himself a glass of brandy
which he downs at one go. He puts the bottle and glass back in place.
He coughs. His cough seems to worry him; he coughs again and
listens hard to the sound. He looks at himself again in the mirror,
coughing, then opens the window; the panting of the animals
becomes louder; he coughs again.]* No, it's not the same! *[He
calms down, shuts the window, feels his bandaged forehead, goes to
his divan, and seems to fall asleep.]*

> *[DUDARD is seen mounting the top stairs; he gets to the landing
> and knocks on BERENGER's door.]*

BERENGER: *[starting up]* What is it?

DUDARD: I've dropped by to see you, Berenger.

BERENGER: Who is it?

DUDARD: It's me.

BERENGER: Who's me?

DUDARD: Me, Dudard.

BERENGER: Ah, it's you, come in!

DUDARD: I hope I'm not disturbing you. *[He tries to open the
door.]* The door's locked.

BERENGER: Just a moment. Oh dear, dear! *[He opens the door.
DUDARD enters.]*

DUDARD: Hello Berenger.

BERENGER: Hello Dudard, what time is it?

DUDARD: So, you're still barricaded in your room! Feeling any
better, old man?

BERENGER: Forgive me, I didn't recognize your voice. *[Goes to
open the window.]* Yes, yes, I think I'm a bit better.

DUDARD: My voice hasn't changed. I recognized yours easily
enough.

BERENGER: I'm sorry, I thought that . . . you're right, your voice is quite normal. Mine hasn't changed either, has it?

DUDARD: Why should it have changed?

BERENGER: I'm not a bit . . . a bit hoarse, am I?

DUDARD: Not that I notice.

BERENGER: That's good. That's very reassuring.

DUDARD: Why, what's the matter with you?

BERENGER: I don't know—does one ever know? Voices can suddenly change—they do change, alas!

DUDARD: Have you caught cold, as well?

BERENGER: I hope not . . . I sincerely hope not. But do sit down, Dudard, take a seat. Sit in the armchair.

DUDARD: [*sitting in the armchair*] Are you still feeling a bit off colour? Is your head still bad? [*He points to* BERENGER's *bandage.*]

BERENGER: Oh yes, I've still got a headache. But there's no bump, I haven't knocked myself . . . have I? [*He lifts the bandage, shows his forehead to* DUDARD.]

DUDARD: No, there's no bump as far as I can see.

BERENGER: I hope there never will be. Never.

DUDARD: If you don't knock yourself, why should there be?

BERENGER: If you really don't want to knock yourself, you don't.

DUDARD: Obviously. One just has to take care. But what's the matter with you? You're all nervous and agitated. It must be your migraine. You just stay quiet and you'll feel better.

BERENGER: Migraine! Don't talk to me about migraines! Don't talk about them!

DUDARD: It's understandable that you've got a migraine after all that emotion.

BERENGER: I can't seem to get over it!

DUDARD: Then it's not surprising you've got a headache.

BERENGER: [*darting to the mirror, lifting the bandage*] Nothing there . . . You know, it can all start from something like that.

DUDARD: What can all start?

BERENGER: I'm frightened of becoming someone else.

DUDARD: Calm yourself, now, and sit down. Dashing up and down the room like that can only make you more nervous.

BERENGER: You're right, I must keep calm. [*He goes and sits down.*] I just can't get over it, you know.

DUDARD: About Jean you mean?—I know.

BERENGER: Yes, Jean, of course—and the others, too.

DUDARD: I realize it must have been a shock to you.

BERENGER: Well, that's not surprising, you must admit.

DUDARD: I suppose so, but you mustn't dramatize the situation; it's no reason for you to . . .

BERENGER: I wonder how you'd have felt. Jean was my best friend. Then to watch him change before my eyes, and the way he got so furious!

DUDARD: I know. You felt let down; I understand. Try and not think about it.

BERENGER: How can I help thinking about it? He was such a warm-hearted person, always so human! Who'd have thought it of him! We'd known each other for . . . for donkey's years. He was the last person I'd have expected to change like that. I felt more sure of him than of myself! And then to do that to me!

DUDARD: I'm sure he didn't do it specially to annoy you!

BERENGER: It seemed as if he did. If you'd seen the state he was in . . . the expression on his face . . .

DUDARD: It's just that you happened to be with him at the time. It would have been the same no matter who was there.

BERENGER: But after all our years together he might have controlled himself in front of me.

DUDARD: You think everything revolves round you, you think that everything that happens concerns you personally; you're not the centre of the universe, you know.

BERENGER: Perhaps you're right. I must try to re-adjust myself, but the phenomenon in itself is so disturbing. To tell the truth, it absolutely shatters me. What can be the explanation?

DUDARD: For the moment I haven't found a satisfactory explanation. I observe the facts, and I take them in. They exist, so they must have an explanation. A freak of Nature, perhaps, some bizarre caprice, an extravagant joke, a game—who knows?

BERENGER: Jean was very proud, of course. I'm not ambitious at all. I'm content to be what I am.

DUDARD: Perhaps he felt an urge for some fresh air, the country, the wide-open spaces . . . perhaps he felt a need to relax. I'm not saying that's any excuse . . .

BERENGER: I understand what you mean, at least I'm trying to. But you know—if someone accused me of being a bad sport, or hopelessly middle class, or completely out of touch with life, I'd still want to stay as I am.

DUDARD: We'll all stay as we are, don't worry. So why get upset over a few cases of rhinoceritis. Perhaps it's just another disease.

BERENGER: Exactly! And I'm frightened of catching it.

DUDARD: Oh stop thinking about it. Really, you attach too much importance to the whole business. Jean's case isn't symptomatic, he's not a typical case—you said yourself he was proud. In my opinion—if you'll excuse me saying this about your friend—he was far too excitable, a bit wild, an eccentric. You mustn't base your judgments on exceptions. It's the average case you must consider.

BERENGER: I'm beginning to see daylight. You see, you couldn't explain this phenomenon to me. And yet you just provided me with a plausible explanation. Yes, of course, he must have been in a critical condition to have got himself into that state. He must have been temporarily unbalanced. And yet he gave his reasons for it, he'd obviously given it a lot of thought, and weighed the pros and cons . . . And what about Boeuf then, was he mad, too . . . ? and what about all the others . . . ?

DUDARD: There's still the epidemic theory. It's like influenza. It's not the first time there's been an epidemic.

BERENGER: There's never been one like this. And what if it's come from the colonies?

DUDARD: In any case you can be sure that Boeuf and the others didn't do what they did—become what they became—just to annoy you. They wouldn't have gone to all that trouble.

BERENGER: That's true, that makes sense, it's a reassuring thought

... or on the other hand, perhaps that makes it worse? [*Rhinoceroses are heard, galloping under the up-stage window.*] There, you hear that? [*He darts to the window.*]

DUDARD: Oh, why can't you leave them alone!

[BERENGER *closes the window again.*]

They're not doing you any harm. Really, you're obsessed by them! It's not good for you. You're wearing yourself out. You've had one shock, why look for more? You just concentrate on getting back to normal.

BERENGER: I wonder if I really am immune?

DUDARD: In any case it's not fatal. Certain illnesses are good for you. I'm convinced this is something you can cure if you want to. They'll get over it, you'll see.

BERENGER: But it's bound to have certain after-effects! An organic upheaval like that can't help but leave ...

DUDARD: It's only temporary, don't you worry.

BERENGER: Are you absolutely certain?

DUDARD: I think so, yes, I suppose so.

BERENGER: But if one really doesn't want to, really doesn't want to catch this thing, which after all is a nervous disease—then you don't catch it, you simply don't catch it! Do you feel like a brandy? [*He goes to the table where the bottle stands.*]

DUDARD: Not for me, thank you, I never touch it. But don't mind me if you want some—you go ahead, don't worry about me. But watch out it doesn't make your headache worse.

BERENGER: Alcohol is good for epidemics. It immunizes you. It kills influenza microbes, for instance.

DUDARD: Perhaps it doesn't kill all microbes. They don't know about rhinoceritis yet.

BERENGER: Jean never touched alcohol. He just pretended to. Maybe that's why he ... perhaps that explains his attitude. [*He offers a full glass to* DUDARD:] You're sure you won't?

DUDARD: No, no, never before lunch, thank you.

[BERENGER *empties his glass, continues to hold it, together with the bottle, in his hands; he coughs.*]

You see, you can't take it. It makes you cough.

BERENGER: [*worried*] Yes, it did make me cough. How did I cough?

DUDARD: Like everyone coughs when they drink something a bit strong.

BERENGER: [*moving to put the glass and bottle back on the table*] There wasn't anything odd about it, was there? It *was* a real human cough?

DUDARD: What are you getting at? It was an ordinary human cough. What other sort of cough could it have been?

BERENGER: I don't know ... Perhaps an animal's cough ... Do rhinoceroses cough?

DUDARD: Look, Berenger, you're being ridiculous, you invent difficulties for yourself, you ask yourself the weirdest questions ... I remember you said yourself that the best protection against the thing was will-power.

BERENGER: Yes, I did.

DUDARD: Well then, prove you've got some.

BERENGER: I have, I assure you ...

DUDARD: Prove it to yourself—now, don't drink any more brandy. You'll feel more sure of yourself then.

BERENGER: You deliberately misunderstand me. I told you the only reason I take it is because it keeps the worst at bay; I'm doing it quite deliberately. When the epidemic's over, then I shall stop drinking. I'd already decided that before the whole business began. I'm just putting it off for the time being!

DUDARD: You're inventing excuses for yourself.

BERENGER: Do you think I am ... ? In any case, that's got nothing to do with what's happening now.

DUDARD: How do we know?

BERENGER: [*alarmed*] Do you really think so? You think that's how the rot sets in? I'm not an alcoholic. [*He goes to the mirror and examines himself.*] Do you think, by any chance ... [*He touches his face, pats his bandaged forehead.*] Nothing's changed; it hasn't done any harm so it must have done good ... or it's harmless at any rate.

DUDARD: I was only joking. I was just teasing you. You see the black side of everything—watch out, or you'll become a neurotic. When you've got over your shock completely and you can get out for a breath of fresh air, you'll feel better— you'll see! All these morbid ideas will vanish.

BERENGER: Go out? I suppose I'll have to. I'm dreading the moment. I'll be bound to meet some of them . . .

DUDARD: What if you do? You only have to keep out of their way. And there aren't as many as all that.

BERENGER: I see them all over the place. You'll probably say that's being morbid, too.

DUDARD: They don't attack you. If you leave them alone, they just ignore you. You can't say they're spiteful. They've even got a certain natural innocence, a sort of frankness. Besides I walked right along the avenue to get to you today. I got here safe and sound, didn't I? No trouble at all.

BERENGER: Just the sight of them upsets me. It's a nervous thing. I don't get angry—no, it doesn't pay to get angry, you never know where it'll lead to, I watch out for that. But it does something to me, here! [He points to his heart.] I get a tight feeling inside.

DUDARD: I think you're right to a certain extent to have some reaction. But you go too far. You've no sense of humour, that's your trouble, none at all. You must learn to be more detached, and try and see the funny side of things.

BERENGER: I feel responsible for everything that happens. I feel involved, I just can't be indifferent.

DUDARD: Judge not lest ye be judged. If you start worrying about everything that happens you'd never be able to go on living.

BERENGER: If only it had happened somewhere else, in some other country, and we'd just read about it in the papers, one could discuss it quietly, examine the question from all points of view and come to an objective conclusion. We could organize debates with professors and writers and lawyers, and blue-stockings and artists and people. And the ordinary man in the street, as well—it would be very interesting and instructive. But when you're involved yourself, when you suddenly find yourself up against the brutal facts you can't help feeling directly concerned—the shock is too violent for you to stay cool and detached. I'm frankly surprised, I'm very very surprised. I can't get over it.

DUDARD: Well I'm surprised, too. Or rather I was. Now I'm starting to get used to it.

BERENGER: Your nervous system is better balanced than mine. You're lucky. But don't you agree it's all very unfortunate ...

DUDARD: [interrupting him] I don't say it's a good thing. And don't get the idea that I'm on the rhinoceroses' side ...

[More sounds of rhinoceroses passing, this time under the down-stage window-frame.]

BERENGER: [with a start] There they are, there they are again! Oh, it's no use, I just can't get used to them. Maybe it's wrong of me, but they obsess me so much in spite of myself, I just can't sleep at night. I get insomnia. I doze a bit in the daytime out of sheer exhaustion.

DUDARD: Take some sleeping tablets.

BERENGER: That's not the answer. If I sleep, it's worse. I dream about them, I get nightmares.

DUDARD: That's what comes of taking things too seriously. You get a kick out of torturing yourself—admit it!

BERENGER: I'm no masochist, I assure you.

DUDARD: Then face the facts and get over it. This is the situation and there's nothing you can do about it.

BERENGER: That's fatalism.

DUDARD: It's common sense. When a thing like this happens there's bound to be a reason for it. That's what we must find out.

BERENGER: [getting up] Well, I don't want to accept the situation.

DUDARD: What else can you do? What are your plans?

BERENGER: I don't know for the moment. I must think it over. I shall write to the papers; I'll draw up manifestos; I shall apply for an audience with the mayor—or his deputy, if the mayor's too busy.

DUDARD: You leave the authorities to act as they think best! I'm not sure if morally you have the right to butt in. In any case, I still think it's not all that serious. I consider it's silly to get worked up because a few people decide to change their skins. They just didn't feel happy in the ones they had. They're free to do as they like.

BERENGER: We must attack the evil at the roots.

DUDARD: The evil! That's just a phrase! Who knows what is evil and what is good? It's just a question of personal preferences. You're worried about your own skin—that's the truth of the matter. But you'll never become a rhinoceros, really you won't . . . you haven't got the vocation!

BERENGER: There you are, you see! If our leaders and fellow citizens all think like you, they'll never take any action.

DUDARD: You wouldn't want to ask for help from abroad, surely? This is an internal affair, it only concerns our country.

BERENGER: I believe in international solidarity . . .

DUDARD: You're a Don Quixote. Oh, I don't mean that nastily, don't be offended! I'm only saying it for your own good, because you really need to calm down.

BERENGER: You're right, I know—forgive me. I get too worked up. But I'll change, I will change. I'm sorry to keep you all this time listening to my ramblings. You must have work to do. Did you get my application for sick leave?

DUDARD: Don't worry about that. It's all in order. In any case, the office hasn't resumed work.

BERENGER: Haven't they repaired the staircase yet? What negligence! That's why everything goes so badly.

DUDARD: They're repairing it now. But it's slow work. It's not easy to find the workmen. They sign on and work for a couple of days, then don't turn up any more. You never see them again. Then you have to look for others.

BERENGER: And they talk about unemployment! At least I hope we're getting a stone staircase.

DUDARD: No, it's wood again, but new wood this time.

BERENGER: Oh! The way these organizations stick to the old

routine. They chuck money down the drain but when it's needed for something really useful they pretend they can't afford it. I bet Mr. Papillon's none too pleased. He was dead set on having a stone staircase. What's he say about it?

DUDARD: We haven't got a Chief any more. Mr. Papillon's resigned.

BERENGER: It's not possible!

DUDARD: It's true, I assure you.

BERENGER: Well, I'm amazed ... Was it on account of the staircase?

DUDARD: I don't think so. Anyway that wasn't the reason he gave.

BERENGER: Why was it then? What got into him?

DUDARD: He's retiring to the country.

BERENGER: Retiring? He's not the age. He might still have become the Director.

DUDARD: He's given it all up! Said he needed a rest.

BERENGER: I bet the management's pretty upset to see him go; they'll have to replace him. All your diplomas should come in useful—you stand a good chance.

DUDARD: I suppose I might as well tell you ... it's really rather funny—the fact is, he turned into a rhinoceros.

[*Distant rhinoceros noises.*]

BERENGER: A rhinoceros!!!! Mr. Papillon a rhinoceros! I can't believe it! I don't think it's funny at all! Why didn't you tell me before?

DUDARD: Well you know you've no sense of humour. I didn't want to tell you ... I didn't want to tell you because I knew very well you wouldn't see the funny side, and it would upset you. You know how impressionable you are!

BERENGER: [*raising his arms to heaven*] Oh that's awful ... Mr. Papillon! And he had such a good job.

DUDARD: That proves his metamorphosis was sincere.

BERENGER: He couldn't have done it on purpose. I'm certain it must have been involuntary.

DUDARD: How can we tell? It's hard to know the real reasons for people's decisions.

BERENGER: He must have made a mistake. He'd got some hidden complexes. He should have been psychoanalysed.

DUDARD: Even if it's a case of dissociation it's still very revealing. It was his way of sublimating himself.

BERENGER: He let himself be talked into it, I feel sure.

DUDARD: That could happen to anybody!

BERENGER: [*alarmed*] To anybody? Oh no, not to you it couldn't —could it? And not to me!

DUDARD: We must hope not.

BERENGER: Because we don't want to . . . that's so, isn't it? Tell me, that *is* so, isn't it?

DUDARD: Yes, yes, of course . . .

BERENGER: [*a little calmer*] I still would have thought Mr. Papillon would have had the strength to resist. I thought he had a bit more character! Particularly as I fail to see where his interest lay—what possible material or moral interest . . .

DUDARD: It was obviously a disinterested gesture on his part.

BERENGER: Obviously. There were extenuating circumstances . . . or were they aggravating? Aggravating, I should think, because if he did it from choice . . . You know, I feel sure that Botard must have taken a very poor view of it—what did he think of his Chief's behaviour?

DUDARD: Oh poor old Botard was quite indignant, absolutely outraged. I've rarely seen anyone so incensed.

BERENGER: Well for once I'm on his side. He's a good man after all. A man of sound common sense. And to think I misjudged him.

DUDARD: He misjudged you, too.

BERENGER: That proves how objective I'm being now. Besides, you had a pretty bad opinion of him yourself.

DUDARD: I wouldn't say I had a bad opinion. I admit I didn't often agree with him. I never liked his scepticism, the way he was always so incredulous and suspicious. Even in this instance I didn't approve of him entirely.

BERENGER: This time for the opposite reasons.

DUDARD: No, not exactly—my own reasoning and my judgment are a bit more complex than you seem to think. It was because

there was nothing precise or objective about the way Botard
argued. I don't approve of the rhinoceroses myself, as you
know—not at all, don't go thinking that! But Botard's attitude
was too passionate, as usual, and therefore over-simplified. His
stand seems to me entirely dictated by hatred of his superiors.
That's where he gets his inferiority complex and his resentment. What's more he talks in clichés, and commonplace
arguments leave me cold.

BERENGER: Well forgive me, but this time I'm in complete
agreement with Botard. He's somebody worthwhile.

DUDARD: I don't deny it, but that doesn't mean anything.

BERENGER: He's a very worthwhile person—and they're not easy
to find these days. He's down-to-earth, with four feet planted
firmly on the ground—I mean, both feet. I'm in complete
agreement with him, and I'm proud of it. I shall congratulate
him when I see him. I deplore Mr. Papillon's action; it was his
duty not to succumb.

DUDARD: How intolerant you are! Maybe Papillon felt the need
for a bit of relaxation after all these years of office life.

BERENGER: [*ironically*] And you're too tolerant, far too broad-
minded!

DUDARD: My dear Berenger, one must always make an effort to
understand. And in order to understand a phenomenon and
its effects you need to work back to the initial causes, by honest
intellectual effort. We must try to do this because, after all,
we are thinking beings. I haven't yet succeeded, as I told you,
and I don't know if I shall succeed. But in any case one has to
start out favourably disposed—or at least, impartial; one has
to keep an open mind—that's essential to a scientific mentality.
Everything is logical. To understand is to justify.

BERENGER: You'll be siding with the rhinoceroses before long.

DUDARD: No, no, not at all. I wouldn't go that far. I'm simply
trying to look the facts unemotionally in the face. I'm trying
to be realistic. I also contend that there is no real evil in what
occurs naturally. I don't believe in seeing evil in everything.
I leave that to the inquisitors.

BERENGER: And you consider all this natural?

DUDARD: What could be more natural than a rhinoceros?

BERENGER: Yes, but for a man to turn into a rhinoceros is abnormal beyond question.

DUDARD: Well, of course, that's a matter of opinion . . .

BERENGER: It is beyond question, absolutely beyond question!

DUDARD: You seem very sure of yourself. Who can say where the normal stops and the abnormal begins? Can you personally define these conceptions of normality and abnormality? Nobody has solved this problem yet, either medically or philosophically. You ought to know that.

BERENGER: The problem may not be resolved philosophically— but in practice it's simple. They may prove there's no such thing as movement . . . and then you start walking . . . [*He starts walking up and down the room.*] . . . and you go on walking, and you say to yourself, like Galileo, 'E pur si muove'. . .

DUDARD: You're getting things all mixed up! Don't confuse the issue. In Galileo's case it was the opposite: theoretic and scientific thought proving itself superior to mass opinion and dogmatism.

BERENGER: [*quite lost*] What does all that mean? Mass opinion, dogmatism—they're just words! I may be mixing everything up in my head but you're losing yours. You don't know what's normal and what isn't any more. I couldn't care less about Galileo . . . I don't give a damn about Galileo.

DUDARD: You brought him up in the first place and raised the whole question, saying that practice always had the last word. Maybe it does, but only when it proceeds from theory! The history of thought and science proves that.

BERENGER: [*more and more furious*] It doesn't prove anything of the sort! It's all gibberish, utter lunacy!

DUDARD: There again we need to define exactly what we mean by lunacy . . .

BERENGER: Lunacy is lunacy and that's all there is to it! Everybody knows what lunacy is. And what about the rhinoceroses —are they practice or are they theory?

DUDARD: Both!

BERENGER: How do you mean—both?

DUDARD: Both the one and the other, or one or the other. It's a debatable point!

BERENGER: Well in that case . . . I refuse to think about it!

DUDARD: You're getting all het up. Our opinions may not exactly coincide but we can still discuss the matter peaceably. These things should be discussed.

BERENGER: [*distracted*] You think I'm getting all het up, do you? I might be Jean. Oh no, no, I don't want to become like him. I mustn't be like him. [*He calms down.*] I'm not very well up in philosophy. I've never studied; you've got all sorts of diplomas. That's why you're so at ease in discussion, whereas I never know what to answer—I'm so clumsy. [*Louder rhinoceros noises passing first under the up-stage window and then the down-stage.*] But I do feel you're in the wrong . . . I feel it instinc-tively—no, that's not what I mean, it's the rhinoceros which has instinct—I feel it intuitively, yes, that's the word, in-tuitively.

DUDARD: What do you understand by 'intuitive'?

BERENGER: Intuitively means . . . well, just like that! I feel it, just like that. I think your excessive tolerance, and your generous indulgence . . . believe me, they're really only weakness . . . just blind spots . . .

DUDARD: You're innocent enough to think that.

BERENGER: You'll always be able to dance rings round me. But, you know what? I'm going to try and get hold of the Logician . . .

DUDARD: What logician?

BERENGER: The Logician, the philosopher, a logician, you know . . . you know better than I do what a logician is. A logician I met, who explained to me . . .

DUDARD: What did he explain to you?

BERENGER: He explained that the Asiatic rhinoceroses were African and the African ones Asiatic.

DUDARD: I don't follow you.

BERENGER: No . . . no . . . he proved the contrary—that the African ones were Asiatic and the Asiatic ones . . . I know what I mean. That's not what I wanted to say. But you'll get on very well with him. He's your sort of person, a very good man, a very subtle mind, brilliant.

[*Increasing noises from the rhinoceroses. The words of the two men are drowned by the animals passing under the windows; for a few moments the lips of* DUDARD *and* BERENGER *are seen to move without any words being heard.*]

There they go again! Will they never stop! [*He runs to the up-stage window.*] Stop it! Stop it! You devils!

[*The rhinoceroses move away.* BERENGER *shakes his fist after them.*]

DUDARD: [*seated*] I'd be happy to meet your Logician. If he can enlighten me on these obscure and delicate points, I'd be only too delighted.

BERENGER: [*as he runs to the down-stage window*] Yes, I'll bring him along, he'll talk to you. He's a very distinguished person, you'll see. [*To the rhinoceroses, from the window.*] You devils! [*Shakes his fist as before.*]

DUDARD: Let them alone. And be more polite. You shouldn't talk to people like that . . .

BERENGER: [*still at the window*] There they go again!

[*A boater pierced by a rhinoceros horn emerges from the orchestra pit under the window and passes swiftly from left to right.*]

There's a boater impaled on a rhinoceros horn. Oh, it's the Logician's hat! It's the Logician's! That's the bloody limit! The Logician's turned into a rhinoceros!

DUDARD: That's no reason to be coarse!

BERENGER: Dear Lord, who can you turn to—who? I ask you! The Logician a rhinoceros!

DUDARD: [*going to the window*] Where is he?

BERENGER: [*pointing*] There, that one there, you see!

DUDARD: He's the only rhinoceros in a boater! That makes you think. You're sure it's your Logician?

BERENGER: The Logician . . . a rhinoceros!!!

DUDARD: He's still retained a vestige of his old individuality.

BERENGER: [*shakes his fist again at the straw-hatted rhinoceros, which has disappeared*] I'll never join up with you! Not me!

DUDARD: If he was a genuine thinker, as you say, he couldn't have got carried away. He must have weighed all the pros and and cons before deciding.

BERENGER: [*still shouting after the ex-Logician and the other rhino-ceroses who have moved away*] I'll never join up with you!

DUDARD: [*settling into the armchair*] Yes, that certainly makes you think!

[BERENGER *closes the down-stage window; goes to the up-stage window where other rhinoceroses are passing, presumably making a tour of the house. He opens the window and shouts:*]

BERENGER: No, I'll never join up with you!

DUDARD: [*aside, in his armchair*] They're going round and round the house. They're playing! Just big babies!

[DAISY *has been seen mounting the top stairs. She knocks on* BERENGER'S *door. She is carrying a basket.*]

There's somebody at the door, Berenger!

[*He takes* BERENGER, *who is still at the window, by the sleeve.*]

BERENGER: [*shouting after the rhinoceroses*] It's a disgrace, mas-querading like this, a disgrace!

DUDARD: There's someone knocking, Berenger, can't you hear?

BERENGER: Open, then, if you want to! [*He continues to watch the rhinoceroses whose noise is fading away.*]

[DUDARD *goes to open the door.*]

DAISY: [*coming in*] Morning, Mr. Dudard.

DUDARD: Oh, it's you, Miss Daisy.

DAISY: Is Berenger here, is he any better?

DUDARD: How nice to see you, my dear. Do you often visit Berenger?

DAISY: Where is he?

DUDARD: [*pointing*] There.

DAISY: He's all on his own, poor thing. And he's not very well at the moment, somebody has to give him a hand.

DUDARD: You're a good friend, Miss Daisy.

DAISY: That's just what I am, a good friend.

DUDARD: You've got a warm heart.

DAISY: I'm a good friend, that's all.

BERENGER: [*turning, leaving the window open*] Oh Miss Daisy! How kind of you to come, how very kind!

DUDARD: It certainly is.

BERENGER: Did you know, Miss Daisy, that the Logician is a rhinoceros?

DAISY: Yes, I did. I caught sight of him in the street as I arrived. He was running very fast for someone his age! Are you feeling any better, Mr. Berenger?

BERENGER: My head's still bad! Still got a headache! Isn't it frightful? What do you think about it?

DAISY: I think you ought to be resting ... you should take things quietly for a few more days.

DUDARD: [*to* BERENGER *and* DAISY] I hope I'm not disturbing you!

BERENGER: [*to* DAISY] I meant about the Logician ...

DAISY: [*to* DUDARD] Why should you be? [*To* BERENGER:] Oh, about the Logician? I don't think anything at all!

DUDARD: [*to* DAISY] I thought I might be in the way!

DAISY: [*to* BERENGER] What do you expect me to think? [*To both:*] I've got some news for you: Botard's a rhinoceros!

DUDARD: Well, well!

BERENGER: I don't believe it. He was against it. You must be mistaken. He protested. Dudard has just been telling me. Isn't that so, Dudard?

DUDARD: That is so.

DAISY: I know he was against it. But it didn't stop him turning, twenty-four hours after Mr. Papillon.

DUDARD: Well, he must have changed his mind! Everybody has the right to do that.

BERENGER: Then obviously anything can happen!

DUDARD: [*to* BERENGER] He was a very good man according to you just now.

BERENGER: [*to* DAISY] I just can't believe you. They must have lied to you.

DAISY: I saw him do it.

BERENGER: Then he must have been lying; he was just pretending.

DAISY: He seemed very sincere; sincerity itself.

BERENGER: Did he give any reasons?

DAISY: What he said was: we must move with the times! Those were his last human words.

DUDARD: [*to* DAISY] I was almost certain I'd meet you here, Miss Daisy.

BERENGER: ... Move with the times! What a mentality! [*He makes a wide gesture.*]

DUDARD: [*to* DAISY] Impossible to find you anywhere else, since the office closed.

BERENGER: [*continuing, aside*] What childishness! [*He repeats the same gesture.*]

DAISY: [*to* DUDARD] If you wanted to see me, you only had to telephone.

DUDARD: [*to* DAISY] Oh you know me, Miss Daisy, I'm discretion itself.

BERENGER: But now I come to think it over, Botard's behaviour doesn't surprise me. His firmness was only a pose. Which doesn't stop him from being a good man, of course. Good men make good rhinoceroses, unfortunately. It's because they are so good that they get taken in.

DAISY: Do you mind if I put this basket on the table? [*She does so.*]

BERENGER: But he was a good man with a lot of resentment ...

DUDARD: [*to* DAISY, *and hastening to help her with the basket*] Excuse me, excuse us both, we should have given you a hand before.

BERENGER: [*continues*] ... He was riddled with hatred for his superiors, and he'd got an inferiority complex ...

DUDARD: [*to* BERENGER] Your argument doesn't hold water, because the example he followed was the Chief's, the very instrument of the people who exploited him, as he used to say. No, it seems to me that with him it was a case of community spirit triumphing over his anarchic impulses.

BERENGER: It's the rhinoceroses which are anarchic, because they're in the minority.

DUDARD: They are, it's true—for the moment.

DAISY: They're a pretty big minority, and getting bigger all the time. My cousin's a rhinoceros now, and his wife. Not to mention leading personalities like the Cardinal de Retz . . .

DUDARD: A prelate!

DAISY: Mazarin.

DUDARD: This is going to spread to other countries, you'll see.

BERENGER: And to think it all started with us!

DAISY: . . . and some of the aristocracy. The Duke of St. Simon.

BERENGER: [with uplifted arms] All our great names!

DAISY: And others, too. Lots of others. Maybe a quarter of the whole town.

BERENGER: We're still in the majority. We must take advantage of that. We must do something before we're inundated.

DUDARD: They're very potent, very.

DAISY: Well for the moment, let's eat. I've brought some food.

BERENGER: You're very kind, Miss Daisy.

DUDARD: [aside] Very kind indeed.

BERENGER: I don't know how to thank you.

DAISY: [to DUDARD] Would you care to stay with us?

DUDARD: I don't want to be a nuisance.

DAISY: Whatever do you mean, Mr. Dudard? You know very well we'd love you to stay.

DUDARD: Well, you know, I'd hate to be in the way . . .

BERENGER: Of course, stay, Dudard. It's always a pleasure to talk to you.

DUDARD: As a matter of fact I'm in a bit of a hurry. I have an appointment.

BERENGER: Just now you said you had nothing to do.

DAISY: [unpacking her basket] You know, I had a lot of trouble finding food. The shops have been plundered; they just devour everything. And a lot of the shops are closed. It's written up outside: 'Closed on account of transformation.'

BERENGER: They should be all rounded up in a big enclosure, and kept under strict supervision.

DUDARD: That's easier said than done. The animals' protection league would be the first to object.

DAISY: And besides everyone has a close relative or a friend among them, and that would make it even more difficult.

BERENGER: So everybody's mixed up in it!

DUDARD: Everybody's in the same boat!

BERENGER: But how can people be rhinoceroses? It doesn't bear thinking about! [*To* DAISY:] Shall I help you lay the table?

DAISY: No, don't bother. I know where the plates are. [*She goes to a cupboard and takes out the plates.*]

DUDARD: [*aside*] She's obviously very familiar with the place . . .

DAISY: [*to* DUDARD] I'm laying for three—all right? You are staying with us?

BERENGER: [*to* DUDARD] Yes, of course you're staying.

DAISY: [*to* BERENGER] You get used to it, you know. Nobody seems surprised any more to see herds of rhinoceroses galloping through the streets. They just stand aside, and then carry on as if nothing had happened.

DUDARD: It's the wisest course to take.

BERENGER: Well I can't get used to it.

DUDARD: [*reflectively*] I wonder if one oughtn't to give it a try?

DAISY: Well right now, let's have lunch.

BERENGER: I don't see how a legal man like yourself can . . .

[*A great noise of rhinoceroses travelling very fast is heard outside. Trumpets and drums are also heard.*]

What's going on?

[*They rush to the down-stage window.*]

What is it?

[*The sound of a wall crumbling is heard. Dust covers part of the stage, enveloping , if possible, the characters. They are heard speaking through it.*]

BERENGER: You can't see a thing! What's happening?

DUDARD: You can't see, but you can hear all right.

BERENGER: That's no good!

DAISY: The plates will be all covered in dust.

BERENGER: How unhygienic!

DAISY: Let's hurry up and eat. We won't pay any attention to them.

[*The dust disperses.*]

BERENGER: [*pointing into the auditorium*] They've demolished the walls of the Fire Station.

DUDARD: That's true, they've demolished them!

DAISY: [*who after moving from the window to near the table holding the plate which she is endeavouring to clean, rushes to join the other two*] They're coming out.

BERENGER: All the firemen, a whole regiment of rhinoceroses, led by drums.

DAISY: They're pouring up the streets!

BERENGER: It's gone too far, much too far!

DAISY: More rhinoceroses are streaming out of the courtyard.

BERENGER: And out of the houses ...

DUDARD: And the windows as well!

DAISY: They're joining up with the others.

[*A man comes out of the landing door left and dashes downstairs at top speed; then another with a large horn on his nose; then a woman wearing an entire rhinoceros head.*]

DUDARD: There aren't enough of us left any more.

BERENGER: How many with one horn, and how many with two?

DUDARD: The statisticians are bound to be compiling statistics now. There'll be plenty of erudite controversy you can be sure!

BERENGER: They can only calculate approximately. It's all happening so fast. It leaves them no time. No time to calculate.

DAISY: The best thing is to let the statisticians get on with it. Come and eat, my dear. That'll calm you down. You'll feel better afterwards. [*To* DUDARD:] And you, too.

[*They move away from the window.* DAISY *takes* BERENGER'S *arm; he allows himself to be led docilely.* DUDARD *suddenly halts.*]

DUDARD: I don't feel very hungry—or rather, to be frank, I don't like tinned food very much. I feel like eating outside on the grass.

BERENGER: You mustn't do that. Think of the risk!

DUDARD: But really I don't want to put you to the trouble.

BERENGER: But we've already told you . . .

DUDARD: [*interrupting* BERENGER] I really mean it.

DAISY: [*to* DUDARD] Of course if you really don't want to stay, we can't force you . . .

DUDARD: I didn't mean to offend you.

BERENGER: [*to* DAISY] Don't let him go, he mustn't go.

DAISY: I'd like him to stay . . . but people must do as they please.

BERENGER: [*to* DUDARD] Man is superior to the rhinoceros.

DUDARD: I didn't say he wasn't. But I'm not with you absolutely either. I don't know; only experience can tell.

BERENGER: [*to* DUDARD] You're weakening too, Dudard. It's just a passing phase which you'll regret.

DAISY: If it's just a passing phase then there's no great danger.

DUDARD: I feel certain scruples! I feel it's my duty to stick by my employers and my friends, through thick and thin.

BERENGER: It's not as if you were married to them.

DUDARD: I've renounced marriage. I prefer the great universal family to the little domestic one.

DAISY: [*softly*] We shall miss you a lot, Dudard, but we can't do anything about it.

DUDARD: It's my duty to stick by them; I have to do my duty.

BERENGER: No you're wrong, your duty is to . . . you don't see where your real duty lies . . . your duty is to oppose them, with a firm, clear mind.

DUDARD: I shall keep my mind clear. [*He starts to move round the stage in circles.*] As clear as ever it was. But if you're going to criticize, it's better to do so from the inside. I'm not going to abandon them. I won't abandon them.

DAISY: He's very good-hearted.

BERENGER: He's too good-hearted. [*To* DUDARD, *then dashing to the door:*] You're too good-hearted, you're human. [*To* DAISY:] Don't let him go. He's making a mistake. He's human.

DAISY: What can I do?

[DUDARD *opens the door and runs off; he goes down the stairs at top speed followed by* BERENGER *who shouts after him from the landing.*]

BERENGER: Come back, Dudard! We're fond of you, don't go! It's too late! [*He comes back.*] Too late!

DAISY: We couldn't do anything. [*She closes the door behind* BERENGER, *who darts to the down-stage window.*]

BERENGER: He's joined up with them. Where is he now?

DAISY: [*moving to the window*] With them.

BERENGER: Which one is he?

DAISY: You can't tell. You can't recognize him any more.

BERENGER: They all look alike, all alike. [*To* DAISY:] He *did* hesitate. You should have held him back by force.

DAISY: I didn't dare to.

BERENGER: You should have been firmer with him, you should have insisted; he was in love with you, wasn't he?

DAISY: He never made me any official declaration.

BERENGER: Everybody knew he was. He's done this out of thwarted love. He was a shy man. He wanted to make a big gesture to impress you. Don't you feel like going after him?

DAISY: Not at all. Or I wouldn't be here!

BERENGER: [*looking out of the window*] You can see nothing but them in the street. [*He darts to the up-stage window.*] Nothing but them! You were wrong, Daisy. [*He looks through the down-stage window again.*] Not a single human being as far as the eye can see. They're all over the street. Half with one horn and half with two, and that's the only distinction!

[*Powerful noises of moving rhinoceroses are heard, but somehow it is a musical sound. On the up-stage wall stylized heads appear and disappear; they become more and more numerous from now on until the end of the play. Towards the end they stay fixed for longer and longer, until eventually they fill the entire back wall, remaining static. The heads, in spite of their monstrous appearance, seem to become more and more beautiful.*]

You don't feel let down, do you, Daisy? There's nothing you regret?

DAISY: No, no.

BERENGER: I want so much to be a comfort to you. I love you, Daisy; don't ever leave me.

DAISY: Shut the window, darling. They're making such a noise. And the dust is rising even up to here. Everything will get filthy.

BERENGER: Yes, you're right. [*He closes the down-stage window and* DAISY *closes the up-stage one. They meet centre-stage.*] I'm not afraid of anything as long as we're together. I don't care what happens. You know, Daisy, I thought I'd never be able to fall in love again. [*He takes her hands, strokes her arms.*]

DAISY: Well you see, everything is possible.

BERENGER: I want so much to make you happy. Do you think you can be happy with me.

DAISY: Why not? If you're happy, then I'll be happy, too. You say nothing scares you, but you're really frightened of everything. What can possibly happen to us?

BERENGER: [*stammering*] My love, my dear love . . . let me kiss your lips. I never dreamed I could still feel such tremendous emotion!

DAISY: You must be more calm and more sure of yourself, now.

BERENGER: I am; let me kiss you.

DAISY: I'm very tired, dear. Stay quiet and rest yourself. Sit in the armchair.

[BERENGER, *led by* DAISY, *sits in the armchair.*]

BERENGER: There was no point in Dudard quarrelling with Botard, as things turned out.

DAISY: Don't think about Dudard any more. I'm here with you. We've no right to interfere in other people's lives.

BERENGER: But you're interfering in mine. You know how to be firm with me.

DAISY: That's not the same thing; I never loved Dudard.

BERENGER: I see what you mean. If he'd stayed he'd always have been an obstacle between us. Ah, happiness is such an egotistical thing!

DAISY: You have to fight for happiness, don't you agree?

BERENGER: I adore you, Daisy; I admire you as well.

DAISY: Maybe you won't say that when you get to know me better.

BERENGER: The more I know you the better you seem; and you're so beautiful, so very beautiful. [*More rhinoceroses are heard passing.*] Particularly compared to them . . . [*He points to the window.*] You probably think that's no compliment, but they make you seem more beautiful than ever . . .

DAISY: Have you been good today? You haven't had any brandy?

BERENGER: Oh yes, I've been good.

DAISY: Is that the truth?

BERENGER: Yes, it's the truth I assure you.

DAISY: Can I believe you, I wonder?

BERENGER: [*a little flustered*] Oh yes, you must believe me.

DAISY: Well all right then, you can have a little glass. It'll buck you up.

    [BERENGER *is about to leap up.*]

    You stay where you are, dear. Where's the bottle?

BERENGER: [*pointing to it*] There, on the little table.

DAISY: [*going to the table and getting the bottle and glass*] You've hidden it well away.

BERENGER: It's out of the way of temptation.

DAISY: [*pours a small glass and gives it to* BERENGER] You've been a good boy. You're making progress.

BERENGER: I'll make a lot more now I'm with you.

DAISY: [*handing him the glass*] Here you are. That's your reward.

BERENGER: [*downing it at one go*] Thank you. [*He holds up his empty glass to* DAISY.]

DAISY: Oh no, dear. That's enough for this morning. [*She takes his glass, puts it back on the table with the bottle.*] I don't want it to make you ill. [*She comes back to him.*] How's your head feel now?

BERENGER: Much better, darling.

DAISY: Then we'll take off the bandage. It doesn't suit you at all.

BERENGER: Oh no, don't touch it.

DAISY: Nonsense, we'll take it off now.

BERENGER: I'm frightened there might be something underneath.

DAISY: [*removing the bandage in spite of his protests*] Always frightened, aren't you, always imagining the worst! There's nothing there, you see. Your forehead's as smooth as a baby's.

BERENGER: [*feeling his brow*] You're right; you're getting rid of my complexes. [DAISY *kisses him on the brow.*] What should I do without you?

DAISY: I'll never leave you alone again.

BERENGER: I won't have any more fears now I'm with you.

DAISY: I'll keep them all at bay.

BERENGER: We'll read books together. I'll become clever.

DAISY: And when there aren't so many people about we'll go for long walks.

BERENGER: Yes, along the Seine, and in the Luxembourg Gardens . . .

DAISY: And to the Zoo.

BERENGER: I'll be brave and strong. I'll keep you safe from harm.

DAISY: You won't need to defend me, silly! We don't wish anyone any harm. And no one wishes us any, my dear.

BERENGER: Sometimes one does harm without meaning to, or rather one allows it to go unchecked. I know you didn't like poor old Mr. Papillon very much—but perhaps you shouldn't have spoken to him so harshly that day when Boeuf turned into a rhinoceros. You needn't have told him he had such horny hands.

DAISY: But it was true—he had!

BERENGER: I know he had, my dear. But you could have said so less bluntly and not hurt his feelings so much. It had a big effect on him.

DAISY: Do you think so?

BERENGER: He didn't show it—he was too proud for that—but the remark certainly went home. It must have influenced his decision. Perhaps you might have been the means of saving him.

DAISY: I couldn't possibly foresee what was going to happen to him . . . besides he was so ill-mannered.

BERENGER: For my own part, I shall never forgive myself for not being nicer to Jean. I never managed to give him a really solid proof of the friendship I felt for him. I wasn't sufficiently understanding with him.

DAISY: Don't worry about it. You did all you could. Nobody can do the impossible. There's no point in reproaching yourself now. Stop thinking about all those people. Forget about them. You must forget all those bad memories.

BERENGER: But they keep coming back to me. They're very real memories.

DAISY: I never knew you were such a realist—I thought you were more poetic. Where's your imagination? There are many sides to reality. Choose the one that's best for you. Escape into the world of the imagination.

BERENGER: It's easy to say that!

DAISY: Aren't I enough for you?

BERENGER: Oh yes, more than enough!

DAISY: You'll spoil everything if you go on having a bad conscience. Everybody has their faults, but you and I have got less than a lot of people.

BERENGER: Do you really think so?

DAISY: We're comparatively better than most. We're good, both of us.

BERENGER: That's true, you're good and I'm good. That's true.

DAISY: Well then we have the right to live. We even owe ourselves a duty to be happy in spite of everything. Guilt is a dangerous symptom. It shows a lack of purity.

BERENGER: You're right, it can lead to that . . . [He points to the window under which the rhinoceroses are passing and to the up-stage wall where another rhinoceros head appears.] . . . a lot of them started like that!

DAISY: We must try and not feel guilty any more.

BERENGER: How right you are, my wonderful love . . . You're

all my happiness; the light of my life ... We are together, aren't we? No one can separate us. Our love is the only thing that's real. Nobody has the right to stop us from being happy —in fact, nobody could, could they?

[*The telephone rings.*]

Who could that be?

DAISY: [*fearful*] Don't answer.

BERENGER: Why not?

DAISY: I don't know. I just feel it's better not to.

BERENGER: It might be Mr. Papillon, or Botard, or Jean or Dudard ringing to say they've had second thoughts. You did say it was probably only a passing phase.

DAISY: I don't think so. They wouldn't have changed their minds so quickly. They've not had time to think it over. They're bound to give it a fair trial.

BERENGER: Perhaps the authorities have decided to take action at last; maybe they're ringing to ask our help in whatever measures they've decided to adopt.

DAISY: I'd be surprised if it was them.

[*The telephone rings again.*]

BERENGER: It is the authorities, I tell you, I recognize the ring —a long drawn-out ring, I can't ignore an appeal from them. It can't be anyone else. [*He picks up the receiver.*] Hallo? [*Trumpetings are heard coming from the receiver.*] You hear that? Trumpeting! Listen!

[DAISY *puts the telephone to her ear, is shocked by the sound, quickly replaces the receiver.*]

DAISY: [*frightened*] What's going on?

BERENGER: They're playing jokes now.

DAISY: Jokes in bad taste!

BERENGER: You see! What did I tell you?

DAISY: You didn't tell me anything.

BERENGER: I was expecting that; it was just what I'd predicted.

DAISY: You didn't predict anything. You never do. You can only predict things after they've happened.

BERENGER: Oh yes, I can; I can predict things all right.

DAISY: That's not nice of them—in fact it's very nasty. I don't like being made fun of.

BERENGER: They wouldn't dare make fun of you. It's me they're making fun of.

DAISY: And naturally I come in for it as well because I'm with you. They're taking their revenge. But what have we done to them?

[*The telephone rings again.*]

Pull the plug out.

BERENGER: The telephone authorities say you mustn't.

DAISY: Oh you never dare to do anything—and you say you could defend me!

BERENGER: [*darting to the radio*] Let's turn on the radio for the news!

DAISY: Yes, we must find out how things stand!

[*The sound of trumpeting comes from the radio.* BERENGER *peremptorily switches it off. But in the distance other trumpetings, like echoes, can be heard.*]

Things are getting really serious! I tell you frankly, I don't like it! [*She is trembling.*]

BERENGER: [*very agitated*] Keep calm! Keep calm!

DAISY: They've taken over the radio stations!

BERENGER: [*agitated and trembling*] Keep calm, keep calm!

[DAISY *runs to the up-stage window, then to the down-stage window and looks out;* BERENGER *does the same in the opposite order, then the two come and face each other centre-stage.*]

DAISY: It's no joke any longer. They mean business!

BERENGER: There's only them left now; nobody but them. Even the authorities have joined them.

[*They cross to the windows as before, and meet again centre-stage.*]

DAISY: Not a soul left anywhere.

BERENGER: We're all alone, we're left all alone.

DAISY: That's what you wanted.

BERENGER: You mean that's what you wanted!

DAISY: It was you!

BERENGER: You!

[*Noises come from everywhere at once. Rhinoceros heads fill the up-stage wall. From left and right in the house, the noise of rushing feet and the panting breath of the animals. But all these disquieting sounds are nevertheless somehow rhythmical, making a kind of music. The loudest noises of all come from above; a noise of stamp-ing. Plaster falls from the ceiling. The house shakes violently.*]

DAISY: The earth's trembling! [*She doesn't know where to run.*]

BERENGER: No, that's our neighbours, the Perissodactyles! [*He shakes his fist to left and right and above.*] Stop it! You're preventing us from working! Noise is forbidden in these flats! Noise is forbidden!

DAISY: They'll never listen to you!

    [*However the noise does diminish, merely forming a sort of musical background.*]

BERENGER: [*he, too, is afraid*] Don't be frightened, my dear. We're together—you're happy with me, aren't you? It's enough that I'm with you, isn't it? I'll chase all your fears away.

DAISY: Perhaps it's all our own fault.

BERENGER: Don't think about it any longer. We mustn't start feeling remorse. It's dangerous to start feeling guilty. We must just live our lives, and be happy. We have the right to be happy. They're not spiteful, and we're not doing them any harm. They'll leave us in peace. You just keep calm and rest. Sit in the armchair. [*He leads her to the armchair.*] Just keep calm! [DAISY *sits in the armchair.*] Would you like a drop of brandy to pull you together?

DAISY: I've got a headache.

BERENGER: [*taking up his bandage and binding* DAISY's *head*] I love you, my darling. Don't you worry, they'll get over it. It's just a passing phase.

DAISY: They won't get over it. It's for good.

BERENGER: I love you. I love you madly.

DAISY: [*taking off the bandage*] Let things just take their course. What can we do about it?

BERENGER: They've all gone mad. The world is sick. They're all sick.

DAISY: We shan't be the ones to cure them.

BERENGER: How can we live in the same house with them?

DAISY: [*calming down*] We must be sensible. We must adapt ourselves and try and get on with them.

BERENGER: They can't understand us.

DAISY: They must. There's no other way.

BERENGER: Do you understand them?

DAISY: Not yet. But we must try to understand the way their minds work, and learn their language.

BERENGER: They haven't got a language! Listen . . . do you call that a language?

DAISY: How do you know? You're no polyglot!

BERENGER: We'll talk about it later. We must have lunch first.

DAISY: I'm not hungry any more. It's all too much. I can't take any more.

BERENGER: But you're the strong one. You're not going to let it get you down. It's precisely for your courage that I admire you so.

DAISY: You said that before.

BERENGER: Do you feel sure of my love?

DAISY: Yes, of course.

BERENGER: I love you so.

DAISY: You keep saying the same thing, my dear.

BERENGER: Listen, Daisy, there *is* something we can do. We'll have children, and our children will have children—it'll take time, but together we can regenerate the human race.

DAISY: Regenerate the human race?

BERENGER: It happened once before.

DAISY: Ages ago. Adam and Eve . . . They had a lot of courage.

BERENGER: And we, too, can have courage. We don't need all that much. It happens automatically with time and patience.

DAISY: What's the use?

BERENGER: Of course we can—with a little bit of courage.

DAISY: I don't want to have children—it's a bore.

BERENGER: How can we save the world, if you don't?

DAISY: Why bother to save it?

BERENGER: What a thing to say! Do it for me, Daisy. Let's save the world.

DAISY: After all, perhaps it's we who need saving. Perhaps we're the abnormal ones.

BERENGER: You're not yourself, Daisy, you've got a touch of fever.

DAISY: There aren't any more of our kind about anywhere, are there?

BERENGER: Daisy, you're not to talk like that!

[DAISY *looks all around at the rhinoceros heads on the walls, on the landing door, and now starting to appear along the footlights.*]

DAISY: Those are the real people. They look happy. They're content to be what they are. They don't look insane. They look very natural. They were right to do what they did.

BERENGER: [*clasping his hands and looking despairingly at* DAISY] We're the ones who are doing right, Daisy, I assure you.

DAISY: That's very presumptuous of you!

BERENGER: You know perfectly well I'm right.

DAISY: There's no such thing as absolute right. It's the world that's right—not you and me.

BERENGER: I *am* right, Daisy. And the proof is that you understand me when I speak to you.

DAISY: What does that prove?

BERENGER: The proof is that I love you as much as it's possible for a man to love a woman.

DAISY: Funny sort of argument!

BERENGER: I don't understand you any longer, Daisy. You don't know what you're saying, darling. Think of our love! Our love . . .

DAISY: I feel a bit ashamed of what you call love—this morbid feeling, this male weakness. And female, too. It just doesn't compare with the ardour and the tremendous energy emanating from all these creatures around us.

BERENGER: Energy! You want some energy, do you? I can let you have some energy! [*He slaps her face.*]

DAISY: Oh! I never would have believed it possible . . . [*She sinks into the armchair.*]

BERENGER: Oh forgive me, my darling, please forgive me! [*He tries to embrace her, she evades him.*] Forgive me, my darling. I didn't mean it. I don't know what came over me, losing control like that!

DAISY: It's because you've run out of arguments, that's why.

BERENGER: Oh dear! In the space of a few minutes we've gone through twenty-five years of married life.

DAISY: I pity you. I understand you all too well ...

BERENGER: [*as* DAISY *weeps*] You're probably right that I've run out of arguments. You think they're stronger than me, stronger than us. Maybe they are.

DAISY: Indeed they are.

BERENGER: Well, in spite of everything, I swear to you I'll never give in, never!

DAISY: [*she rises, goes to* BERENGER, *puts her arms round his neck*] My poor darling, I'll help you to resist—to the very end.

BERENGER: Will you be capable of it?

DAISY: I give you my word. You can trust me.
    [*The rhinoceros noises have become melodious.*]
    Listen, they're singing!

BERENGER: They're not singing, they're roaring.

DAISY: They're singing.

BERENGER: They're roaring, I tell you.

DAISY: You're mad, they're singing.

BERENGER: You can't have a very musical ear, then.

DAISY: You don't know the first thing about music, poor dear— and look, they're playing as well, and dancing.

BERENGER: You call that dancing?

DAISY: It's their way of dancing. They're beautiful.

BERENGER: They're disgusting!

DAISY: You're not to say unpleasant things about them. It upsets me.

BERENGER: I'm sorry. We're not going to quarrel on their account.

DAISY: They're like gods.

BERENGER: You go too far, Daisy; take a good look at them.

DAISY: You mustn't be jealous, my dear.

[*She goes to* BERENGER *again and tries to embrace him. This time it is* BERENGER *who frees himself.*]

BERENGER: I can see our opinions are directly opposed. It's better not to discuss the matter.

DAISY: Now you mustn't be nasty.

BERENGER: Then don't you be stupid!

DAISY: [*to* BERENGER, *who turns his back on her. He looks at himself closely in the mirror*] It's no longer possible for us to live together.

[*As* BERENGER *continues to examine himself in the mirror she goes quietly to the door, saying:*]

He isn't very nice, really, he isn't very nice. [*She goes out, and is seen slowly descending the stairs.*]

BERENGER: [*still looking at himself in the mirror*] Men aren't so bad-looking, you know. And I'm not a particularly handsome specimen! Believe me, Daisy! [*He turns round.*] Daisy! Daisy! Where are you, Daisy? You can't do that to me! [*He darts to the door.*] Daisy! [*He gets to the landing and leans over the banister.*] Daisy! Come back! Come back, my dear! You haven't even had your lunch. Daisy, don't leave me alone! Remember your promise! Daisy! Daisy! [*He stops calling, makes a despairing gesture, and comes back into the room.*] Well, it was obvious we weren't getting along together. The home was broken up. It just wasn't working out. But she shouldn't have left like that with no explanation. [*He looks all around.*] She didn't even leave a message. That's no way to behave. Now I'm all on my own. [*He locks the door carefully, but angrily.*] But they won't get me. [*He carefully closes the windows.*] You won't get me! [*He addresses all the rhinoceros heads.*] I'm not joining you; I don't understand you! I'm staying as I am. I'm a human being. A human being. [*He sits in the armchair.*] It's an impossible situation. It's my fault she's gone. I meant everything to her. What'll become of her? That's one more person on my conscience. I can easily picture the worst, because the worst can easily happen. Poor little thing left all alone in this world of monsters! Nobody can help me find her, nobody, because there's nobody left.

[*Fresh trumpetings, hectic racings, clouds of dust.*]

I can't bear the sound of them any longer, I'm going to put cotton wool in my ears. [*He does so, and talks to himself in the mirror.*] The only solution is to convince them—but convince them of what? Are the changes reversible, that's the point? Are they reversible? It would be a labour of Hercules, far beyond me. In any case, to convince them you'd have to talk to them. And to talk to them I'd have to learn their language. Or they'd have to learn mine. But what language do I speak? What is my language? Am I talking French? Yes, it must be French. But what is French? I can call it French if I want, and nobody can say it isn't—I'm the only one who speaks it. What am I saying? Do I understand what I'm saying? Do I? [*He crosses to the middle of the room.*] And what if it's true what Daisy said, and they're the ones in the right? [*He turns back to the mirror.*] A man's not ugly to look at, not ugly at all! [*He examines himself, passing his hand over his face.*] What a funny-looking thing! What do I look like? What? [*He darts to a cupboard, takes out some photographs which he examines.*] Photographs! Who are all these people? Is it Mr. Papillon—or is it Daisy? And is that Botard or Dudard or Jean? Or is it me? [*He rushes to the cupboard again and takes out two or three pictures.*] Now I recognize me: that's me, that's me! [*He hangs the pictures on the back wall, beside the rhinoceros heads.*] That's me, that's me!

[*When he hangs the pictures one sees that they are of an old man, a huge woman, and another man. The ugliness of these pictures is in contrast to the rhinoceros heads which have become very beautiful.* BERENGER *steps back to contemplate the pictures.*]

I'm not good-looking, I'm not good-looking. [*He takes down the pictures, throws them furiously to the ground, and goes over to the mirror.*] They're the good-looking ones. I was wrong! Oh, how I wish I was like them! I haven't got any horns, more's the pity! A smooth brow looks so ugly. I need one or two horns to give my sagging face a lift. Perhaps one will grow and I needn't be ashamed any more—then I could go and join them. But it will never grow! [*He looks at the palms of his hands.*] My hands are so limp—oh, why won't they get rough! [*He takes his coat off, undoes his shirt to look at his chest in the mirror.*] My skin is so slack. I can't stand this white, hairy body. Oh I'd love to have a hard skin in that wonderful dull green colour—a skin that looks decent naked without any hair on it, like theirs! [*He listens to the trumpetings.*] Their song is charming—a bit raucous perhaps, but it does have charm! I wish I could do it! [*He tries to imitate them.*] Ahh, Ahh, Brr! No, that's not it! Try again, louder! Ahh, Ahh, Brr! No, that's not it, it's too feeble, it's got no drive behind it. I'm not trumpeting at all; I'm just howling. Ahh, Ahh, Brr. There's a big difference between howling and trumpeting. I've only myself to blame; I should have gone with them while there was still time. Now it's too late! Now I'm a monster, just a monster. Now I'll never become a rhinoceros, never, never! I've gone past changing. I want to, I really do, but I can't, I just can't. I can't stand the sight of me. I'm too ashamed! [*He turns his back on the mirror.*] I'm so ugly! People who try to hang on to their individuality always come to a bad end! [*He suddenly snaps out of it.*] Oh well, too bad! I'll take on the whole of them! I'll put up a fight against the lot of them, the whole lot of them! I'm the last man left, and I'm staying that way until the end. I'm not capitulating!

CURTAIN

THE LEADER

THE LEADER

[*Standing with his back to the public, centre-stage, and with his eyes fixed on the up-stage exit, the* ANNOUNCER *waits for the arrival of the* LEADER. *To right and left, riveted to the walls, two of the* LEADER'S ADMIRERS, *a man and a girl, also wait for his arrival.*]

ANNOUNCER: [*after a few tense moments in the same position*] There he is! There he is! At the end of the street! [*Shouts of 'Hurrah!' etc., are heard.*] There's the leader! He's coming, he's coming nearer! [*Cries of acclaim and applause are heard from the wings.*] It's better if he doesn't see us . . . [*The* TWO ADMIRERS *hug the wall even closer.*] Watch out! [*The* ANNOUNCER *gives vent to a brief display of enthusiasm.*] Hurrah! Hurrah! The leader! The leader! Long live the leader! [*The* TWO ADMIRERS, *with their bodies rigid and flattened against the wall, thrust their necks and heads as far forward as they can to get a glimpse of the* LEADER.] The leader! The leader! [*The* TWO ADMIRERS *in unison:*] Hurrah! Hurrah! [*Other 'Hurrahs!' mingled with 'Hurrah! Bravo!' come from the wings and gradually die down.*] Hurrah! Bravo!

[*The* ANNOUNCER *takes a step up-stage, stops, then up-stage, followed by the* TWO ADMIRERS, *saying as he goes:* 'Ah! Too bad! He's going away! He's going away! Follow me quickly!

After him!' The ANNOUNCER *and the* TWO ADMIRERS
leave, crying: 'Leader! Leeeeader! Lee-ee-eader!' *(This last*
'Lee-ee-eader!' *echoes in the wings like a bleating cry.*)]

[*Silence. The stage is empty for a few brief moments. The* YOUNG
LOVER *enters right, and his* GIRL-FRIEND *left; they meet centre-
stage.*]

YOUNG LOVER: Forgive me, Madame, or should I say Mademoi-
selle?

GIRL-FRIEND: I beg your pardon, I'm afraid I don't happen to
know you!

YOUNG LOVER: And I'm afraid I don't know you either!

GIRL-FRIEND: Then neither of us knows each other.

YOUNG LOVER: Exactly. We have something in common. It
means that between us there is a basis of understanding on
which we can build the edifice of our future.

GIRL-FRIEND: That leaves me cold, I'm afraid.

[*She makes as if to go.*]

YOUNG LOVER: Oh, my darling, I adore you.

GIRL-FRIEND: Darling, so do I!

[*They embrace.*]

YOUNG LOVER: I'm taking you with me, darling. We'll get
married straightaway.

[*They leave left. The stage is empty for a brief moment.*]

ANNOUNCER: [*enters up-stage followed by the* TWO ADMIRERS] But
the leader swore that he'd be passing here.

ADMIRER: Are you absolutely sure of that?

ANNOUNCER: Yes, yes, of course.

GIRL ADMIRER: Was it really on his way?

ANNOUNCER: Yes, yes. He should have passed by here, it was
marked on the Festival programme . . .

ADMIRER: Did you actually see it yourself and hear it with your
own eyes and ears?

ANNOUNCER: He told someone. Someone else!

ADMIRER: But who? Who was this someone else?

GIRL ADMIRER: Was it a reliable person? A friend of yours?

ANNOUNCER: A friend of mine who I know very well. [*Suddenly*

*in the background one hears renewed cries of 'Hurrah!' and 'Long
live the leader!'*] That's him now! There he is! Hip! Hip!
Hurrah! There he is! Hide yourselves! Hide yourselves!

[*The* TWO ADMIRERS *flatten themselves as before against the
wall, stretching their necks out towards the wings from where the
shouts of acclamation come; the* ANNOUNCER *watches fixedly up-
stage his back to the public.*]

ANNOUNCER: The leader's coming. He approaches. He's bending.
He's unbending. [*At each of the* ANNOUNCER'S *words, the*
ADMIRERS *give a start and stretch their necks even farther; they
shudder.*] He's jumping. He's crossed the river. They're shaking
his hand. He sticks out his thumb. Can you hear? They're
laughing. [*The* ANNOUNCER *and the* TWO ADMIRERS *also laugh.*]
Ah . . . ! they're giving him a box of tools. What's he going to
do with them? Ah . . . ! he's signing autographs. The leader
is stroking a hedgehog, a superb hedgehog! The crowd
applauds. He's dancing, with the hedgehog in his hand. He's
embracing his dancer. Hurrah! Hurrah! [*Cries are heard in the
wings.*] He's being photographed, with his dancer on one hand
and the hedgehog on the other . . . He greets the crowd . . .
He spits a tremendous distance.

GIRL ADMIRER: Is he coming past here? Is he coming in our
direction?

ADMIRER: Are we really on his route?

ANNOUNCER: [*turns his head to the* TWO ADMIRERS] Quite, and
don't move, you're spoiling everything . . .

GIRL ADMIRER: But even so . . .

ANNOUNCER: Keep quiet, I tell you! Didn't I tell you he'd
promised, that he had fixed his itinerary himself. . . . [*He turns
back up-stage and cries.*] Hurrah! Hurrah! Long live the leader!
[*Silence*] Long live, long live, the leader! [*Silence*] Long live,
long live, long live the lead-er! [*The* TWO ADMIRERS, *unable
to contain themselves, also give a sudden cry of:*] Hurrah! Long live
the leader!

ANNOUNCER: [*to the* ADMIRERS] Quiet, you two! Calm down!
You're spoiling everything! [*Then, once more looking up-stage,*

with the ADMIRERS *silenced*.] Long live the leader! [*Wildly enthusiastic*.] Hurrah! Hurrah! He's changing his shirt. He disappears behind a red screen. He reappears! [*The applause intensifies*.] Bravo! Bravo! [*The* ADMIRERS *also long to cry 'Bravo' and applaud; they put their hands to their mouths to stop themselves*.] He's putting his tie on! He's reading his newspaper and drinking his morning coffee! He's still got his hedgehog ... He's leaning on the edge of the parapet. The parapet breaks. He gets up ... he gets up unaided! [*Applause, shouts of 'Hurrah!'*] Bravo! Well done! He brushes his soiled clothes.

TWO ADMIRERS: [*stamping their feet*] Oh! Ah! Oh! Oh! Ah! Ah!

ANNOUNCER: He's mounting the stool! He's climbing piggy-back, they're offering him a thin-ended wedge, he knows it's meant as a joke, and he doesn't mind, he's laughing.

[*Applause and enormous acclaim*.]

ADMIRER: [*to the* GIRL ADMIRER] You hear that? You hear? Oh! If I were king ...

GIRL ADMIRER: Ah ... ! the leader!

[*This is said in an exalted tone*.]

ANNOUNCER: [*still with his back to the public*] He's mounting the stool. No. He's getting down. A little girl offers him a bouquet of flowers ... What's he going to do? He takes the flowers ... He embraces the little girl ... calls her 'my child'...

ADMIRER: He embraces the little girl ... calls her 'my child'...

GIRL ADMIRER: He embraces the little girl ... calls her 'my child'...

ANNOUNCER: He gives her the hedgehog. The little girl's crying ... Long live the leader! Long live the leead-er!

ADMIRER: Is he coming past here?

GIRL ADMIRER: Is he coming past here?

ANNOUNCER: [*with a sudden run, dashes out up-stage*] He's going away! Hurry! Come on!

[*He disappears, followed by the* TWO ADMIRERS, *all crying 'Hurrah! Hurrah!'*]

[*The stage is empty for a few moments. The* TWO LOVERS *enter*, *entwined in an embrace; they halt centre-stage and separate; she carries a basket on her arm.*]

GIRL-FRIEND: Let's go to the market and get some eggs!

YOUNG LOVER: Oh! I love them as much as you do!

[*She takes his arm. From the right the* ANNOUNCER *arrives running, quickly regaining his place, back to the public, followed closely by the* TWO ADMIRERS, *arriving one from the left and the other from the right; the* TWO ADMIRERS *knock into the* TWO LOVERS *who were about to leave right.*]

ADMIRER: Sorry!

YOUNG LOVER: Oh! Sorry!

GIRL ADMIRER: Sorry! Oh! Sorry!

GIRL-FRIEND: Oh! Sorry, sorry, sorry, so sorry!

ADMIRER: Sorry, sorry, sorry, oh! sorry, sorry, so sorry!

YOUNG LOVER: Oh, oh, oh, oh, oh, oh! So sorry, everyone!

GIRL-FRIEND: [*to her* LOVER] Come along, Adolphe! [*To the* TWO ADMIRERS:] No harm done!

[*She leaves, leading her* LOVER *by the hand.*]

ANNOUNCER: [*watching up-stage*] The leader is being pressed forward, and pressed back, and now they're pressing his trousers! [*The* TWO ADMIRERS *regain their places.*] The leader is smiling. Whilst they're pressing his trousers, he walks about. He tastes the flowers and the fruits growing in the stream. He's also tasting the roots of the trees. He suffers the little children to come unto him. He has confidence in everybody. He inaugurates the police force. He pays tribute to justice. He salutes the great victors and the great vanquished. Finally he recites a poem. The people are very moved.

TWO ADMIRERS: Bravo! Bravo! [*Then, sobbing:*] Boo! Boo! Boo!

ANNOUNCER: All the people are weeping. [*Loud cries are heard from the wings; the* ANNOUNCER *and the* ADMIRERS *also start to bellow.*] Silence! [*The* TWO ADMIRERS *fall silent; and there is silence from the wings.*] They've given the leader's trousers back. The leader puts them on. He looks happy! Hurrah! [*'Bravos', and acclaim from the wings. The* TWO ADMIRERS *also shout their acclaim, jump about, without being able to see anything of what is presumed to be happening in the wings.*] The leader's sucking his thumb! [*To the* Two Admirers:] Back, back to your places, you two, don't move, behave yourselves and shout: 'Long live the leader!'

Two Admirers: [*flattened against the wall, shouting*] Long live, long live the leader!

Announcer: Be quiet, I tell you, you'll spoil everything! Look out, the leader's coming!

Admirer: [*in the same position*] The leader's coming!

Girl Admirer: The leader's coming!

Announcer: Watch out! And keep quiet! Oh! The leader's going away! Follow him! Follow me!

[*The* Announcer *goes out up-stage, running; the* Two Admirers *leave right and left, whilst in the wings the acclaim mounts, then fades. The stage is momentarily empty. The* Young Lover, *followed by his* Girl-Friend, *appear left running across the stage right.*]

Young Lover: [*running*] You won't catch me! You won't catch me!

[*Goes out.*]

Girl-Friend: [*running*] Wait a moment! Wait a moment!

[*She goes out. The stage is empty for a moment; then once more the* Two Lovers *cross the stage at a run, and leave.*]

Young Lover: You won't catch me!

Girl-Friend: Wait a moment!

[*They leave right. The stage is empty. The* Announcer *re-appears up-stage, the* Admirer *from the right, the* Girl Admirer *from the left. They meet centre.*]

Admirer: We missed him!

Girl Admirer: Rotten luck!

Announcer: It was your fault!

Admirer: That's not true!

Girl Admirer: No, that's not true!

Announcer: Are you suggesting it was mine?

Admirer: No, we didn't mean that!

GIRL ADMIRER: No, we didn't mean that!

   [*Noise of acclaim and 'Hurrahs' from the wings.*]

ANNOUNCER: Hurrah!

GIRL ADMIRER: It's from over there! [*She points up-stage.*]

ADMIRER: Yes, it's from over there! [*He points left.*]

ANNOUNCER: Very well. Follow me! Long live the leader!

   [*He runs out right, followed by the* TWO ADMIRERS, *also shouting.*]

TWO ADMIRERS: Long live the leader!

   [*They leave. The stage is empty for a moment. The* YOUNG LOVER *and his* GIRL-FRIEND *appear left; the* YOUNG LOVER *exits up-stage; the* GIRL-FRIEND, *after saying 'I'll get you!', runs out right. The* ANNOUNCER *and the* TWO ADMIRERS *appear from up-stage. The* ANNOUNCER *says to the* ADMIRERS:] Long live the leader! [*This is repeated by the* ADMIRERS. *Then, still talking to the* ADMIRERS, *he says:*] Follow me! Follow the leader! [*He leaves up-stage, still running and shouting:*] Follow him!

   [*The* ADMIRER *exits right, the* GIRL ADMIRER *left into the wings. During the whole of this, the acclaim is heard louder or fainter according to the rhythm of the stage action; the stage is empty for a moment, then the* LOVERS *appear from right and left, crying:*]

YOUNG LOVER: I'll get you!

GIRL-FRIEND: You won't get me!

   [*They leave at a run, shouting:*] Long live the leader! [*The* ANNOUNCER *and the* TWO ADMIRERS *emerge from up-stage, also shouting: 'Long live the leader', followed by the* TWO LOVERS. *They all leave right, in single file, crying as they run: 'The leader! Long live the leader! We'll get him! It's from over here! You won't get me!'*]

   [*They enter and leave, employing all the exits; finally, entering from left, from right, and from up-stage they all meet centre, whilst the acclaim and the applause from the wings becomes a fearful din. They embrace each other feverishly, crying at the tops of their voices:*] Long live the leader! Long live the leader! Long live the leader!

[*Then, abruptly, silence falls.*]

ANNOUNCER: The leader is arriving. Here's the leader. To your places! Attention!

[*The* ADMIRER *and the* GIRL-FRIEND *flatten themselves against the wall right; the* GIRL ADMIRER *and the* YOUNG LOVER *against the wall left; the two couples are in each other's arms, embracing.*]

ADMIRER and
GIRL-FRIEND: My dear, my darling!
GIRL ADMIRER and
YOUNG LOVER: My dear, my darling!

[*Meanwhile the* ANNOUNCER *has taken up his place, back to the audience, looking fixedly up-stage; a lull in the applause.*]

ANNOUNCER: Silence. The leader has eaten his soup. He is coming. He is nigh.

[*The acclaim redoubles its intensity; the* TWO ADMIRERS *and the* TWO LOVERS *shout:*]

ALL: Hurrah! Hurrah! Long live the leader!

[*They throw confetti before he arrives. Then the* ANNOUNCER *hurls himself suddenly to one side to allow the* LEADER *to pass; the other four characters freeze with outstretched arms holding confetti; but still say:*] Hurrah! [*The* LEADER *enters from up-stage, advances down-stage to centre; to the footlights, hesitates, makes a step to left, then takes a decision and leaves with great, energetic strides by right, to the enthusiastic 'Hurrahs!' of the* ANNOUNCER *and the feeble, somewhat astonished 'Hurrahs!' of the other four; these, in fact, have some reason to be surprised, as the* LEADER *is headless, though wearing a hat. This is simple to effect: the actor playing the* LEADER *needing only to wear an overcoat with the collar turned up round his forehead and topped with a hat. The-man-in-an-overcoat-with-a-hat-without-a-head is a somewhat surprising apparition and will doubtless produce a certain sensation. After the* LEADER'S *disappearance, the* GIRL ADMIRER *says:*]

GIRL ADMIRER: But . . . but . . . the leader hasn't got a head!
ANNOUNCER: What's he need a head for when he's got genius!

YOUNG LOVER: That's true! [*To the* GIRL-FRIEND:] What's your name?

[*The* YOUNG LOVER *to the* GIRL ADMIRER, *the* GIRL ADMIRER *to the* ANNOUNCER, *the* ANNOUNCER *to the* GIRL-FRIEND, *the* GIRL-FRIEND *to the* YOUNG LOVER:] What's yours? What's yours? What's yours? [*Then, all together, one to the other:*] What's your name?

CURTAIN

THE FUTURE IS IN EGGS
or
IT TAKES ALL SORTS TO MAKE A WORLD

THE FUTURE IS IN EGGS
or
IT TAKES ALL SORTS TO MAKE A WORLD

CHARACTERS

JACQUES
FATHER-JACQUES
MOTHER-JACQUES
JACQUELINE
GRANDMOTHER-JACQUES
GRANDFATHER-JACQUES
ROBERTA
FATHER-ROBERT
MOTHER-ROBERT

This play constitutes a kind of sequel to

JACQUES OR OBEDIENCE

[*As the curtain rises,* JACQUES *and* ROBERTA *are embracing, squatting in the same position as at the end of* 'JACQUES'; *the change of decor is of no importance.*]
[*Up-stage left there is now a large piece of furniture, a sort of long table or a kind of divan which serves as a hatching apparatus. The picture, 'expressing nothing' on the up-stage wall is replaced in the present scene by a large frame containing a portrait of* GRANDFATHER-JACQUES, *which is to say,* GRANDFATHER-JACQUES *himself. There are chairs around the hatching apparatus. There is a sound of rain.*]
[FATHER- *and* MOTHER-JACQUES, FATHER- *and* MOTHER-ROBERT, JACQUELINE, *and* GRANDMOTHER-JACQUES *are standing round* JACQUES *and* ROBERTA, *looking first at them, then at*

each other, shaking their heads, shrugging their shoulders and
murmuring: 'It's a bit much!']

[Engrossed in each other, JACQUES and ROBERTA do not even see
them.]

ROBERTA: Puss ... Puss ...

JACQUES: Puss ... Puss ...

ROBERTA: Puss ... Puss ...

JACQUES: Puss ... Puss ...

ROBERTA: Puss ... Puuusss ...

JACQUES: Puuuss ... Puuuuuuuuss! ...

[ROBERTA and JACQUES purr. The four parents, the GRAND-
MOTHER and JACQUELINE are not at all pleased. They are heard
to say:]

FATHER-JACQUES: They go too far ...

GRANDMOTHER-JACQUES: All this wasn't necessary in my day ...

FATHER-ROBERT: They really do exaggerate.

MOTHER-ROBERT: [to her husband] It all comes from Jacques, of
course.

MOTHER-JACQUES: [to her husband] Of course it's all Roberta's
fault.

JACQUES: [absorbed in his love] Pusspusspusspusspuuuuusss ...
Pusspusspusspusspuuuuusss ...

ROBERTA and JACQUES: Pusspusspusssss ... [They purr.] Pussy-
pussy ...

FATHER-JACQUES: They're making a proper spectacle of themselves!

JACQUELINE: But, father, you only have to look in the street, and
at the bus-stops—nowadays young people don't seem to care.

MOTHER-ROBERT: Roberta would never dream of making a
spectacle of herself.

MOTHER-JACQUES: It would never cross my son's mind ...

JACQUES and ROBERTA: Pusspusspuss ... Purr ... purr ... purr ...

FATHER-JACQUES: Spectacle or no spectacle, it's the result that
counts ... And all this is leading nowhere!

MOTHER-JACQUES: [to FATHER-JACQUES] Come now, you must
have a little patience, papa ...

GRANDMOTHER-JACQUES: Be practical!

MOTHER-JACQUES: [*to* FATHER-JACQUES] You're in too much of a rush—remember, it was the same with us, we didn't get results straightaway.

ROBERTA and JACQUES: [*embracing*] Pusspusspusspuuusss . . . Purr . . . purr . . . purr . . .

FATHER-JACQUES: You don't need to stick up for them.

GRANDMOTHER-JACQUES: She doesn't take after them at all.

FATHER-ROBERT: [*to his wife*] I never would have stood for it!

MOTHER-ROBERT: [*to her husband*] Now you calm down!

FATHER-JACQUES: Quiet!

MOTHER-JACQUES: Oh, you're always being nasty . . . yet you're always so good!

FATHER-ROBERT: [*to his wife*] Old Mother-Jacques's always bleating about something. Nobody's interested in what she thinks.

MOTHER-ROBERT: [*to her husband*] She ought to keep her mouth shut.

JACQUELINE: [*to the* ROBERT-COUPLE] What did you say?

FATHER-ROBERT: Nothing—that is, we were just saying something nice about you, my dear . . .

ROBERTA and JACQUES: [*still squatting in an embrace*] Puuuussss . . . purrpurrpurr . . .

MOTHER-ROBERT: I think they're rather sweet, the two of them.

FATHER-JACQUES: That's just what I blame them for, in the name of tradition . . . They've been sweet enough, they're far too sweet . . .

JACQUELINE: It's about all they are!

JACQUES and ROBERTA: Pusspuuuuss . . . Purrpurrpurr . . .

FATHER-JACQUES: [*to* FATHER-ROBERT] It's three years now since we arranged this marriage. And they've been stuck there ever since caterwauling, with us watching them. And nothing happens.

MOTHER-JACQUES: In spite of all our good wishes and encouragement.

FATHER-JACQUES: Nothing happens, nothing at all! We must get some results quickly!

FATHER-ROBERT: [*to* FATHER-JACQUES] I'll say again. It's not my daughter's fault.

FATHER-JACQUES: [*to* FATHER-ROBERT] Are you suggesting it's the fault of my son? Is that what you're insinuating?

MOTHER-ROBERT: [*to* FATHER-JACQUES] Now, don't take it like that!

JACQUES and ROBERTA: Puuuuss . . . ! Purrpurrpurr . . .

FATHER-JACQUES: We must come to a decision! Come on, Jacqueline, show some initiative . . .

JACQUES and ROBERTA: Pusspusspusssssss! Purrpurrpurr . . .

JACQUELINE: Why always me! . . . Why can't you all peave me in leace!

FATHER-JACQUES: [*threateningly*] Jacqueline! Jacqueline!! Jacqueline!!! . . .

JACQUELINE: [*with bowed head*] Sorry, papa.

MOTHER-ROBERT: [*to her husband*] And now they're getting on their high horses!

JACQUELINE: [*to* FATHER-JACQUES] I understand, papa. Very well, papa. Whatever you say, papa.

GRANDMOTHER-JACQUES: There's a good child!

MOTHER-JACQUES: My little girl . . . She's my big consolation.

MOTHER-ROBERT: [*to her husband*] That's true enough!

FATHER-ROBERT:
MOTHER-ROBERT:
FATHER-JACQUES:
GRANDMOTHER-JACQUES: } [*holding out their arms to* JACQUELINE, *whilst the portrait of* GRANDFATHER *stays motionless and quiet*] What a good child! What a good child! What a good child!

JACQUELINE: Let's first try and separate them . . . so we can unite them closer afterwards!

[*The parents withdraw slightly. All, including* GRANDFATHER, *follow* JACQUELINE *with their eyes.*]

JACQUELINE: [*to the loving couple*] Glet up!

JACQUES and ROBERTA: Pusspusspuuusss . . . pusspusspuss . . . purrpurrpurr purr . . . purrpurrpurr . . .

JACQUELINE: [*claps her hands.* JACQUES *and* ROBERTA *still fail to hear and continue to purr tenderly in their embrace*] That's enough, do you hear? Enough!!! [*She shakes the couple vigorously.*] Now then! Come on!

[JACQUES *and* ROBERTA *stop their purring, and, as if waking from a deep sleep, look at* JACQUELINE *with surprise, having difficulty in recognizing her in their sleepy state; they get up painfully, looking haggard, still in an embrace.*]

JACQUELINE: [*aside*] Oh, look at her, with her three noses running!

[*Then, with great energy and some sharp taps, she frees their arms and separates them.*]

JACQUELINE: There ... like that ... Straighten yourselves up! ...

[*Murmurs of satisfaction from* JACQUES' *and* ROBERTA's *parents.*]

JACQUES: I'm hungry.

ROBERTA: I'm hungry.

JACQUELINE: You're wet through.

JACQUES: I'm cold. Brrr! I'm trembling!

ROBERTA: I'm cold. Brrr! I'm trembling!

[*They both tremble with cold.*]

JACQUELINE: Serves you right!

FATHER-JACQUES: Serves you right!

JACQUES and ROBERTA: I'm hungry!

MOTHER-ROBERT: Poor things!

FATHER-ROBERT: [*to his wife*] They don't get anything to eat in this house.

JACQUELINE: All you think about is your stomach. You're neglecting production! Why don't you get on with it? After all, it is your main duty.

FATHER-JACQUES:
MOTHER-JACQUES:
GRANDMOTHER-JACQUES: } It's your duty!
MOTHER-ROBERT:
FATHER-ROBERT:

TOG. { JACQUES: [*to* ROBERTA] That's true, my dear ...
{ ROBERTA: [*to* JACQUES] That's true, my dear ...

JACQUES and ROBERTA: It's our duty!

FATHER-JACQUES: [*to* JACQUES *and* ROBERTA] So what about it?

JACQUES: I'm hungry.

ROBERTA: I'm hungry.

MOTHER-JACQUES: Oh, poor darlings [*Moved*] they're hungry!
... Oh, my poor little sweets, my little darlings ...

MOTHER-ROBERT: [*to her husband*] She's good-hearted.

FATHER-ROBERT: [*to his wife*] Don't you start climbing down!
The Roberts have their pride, too, you know.

GRANDMOTHER-JACQUES: [*handing a dish to* JACQUES *and* ROBERTA
into which they can dip with their fingers as she holds it] Here you
are, dears, old granny's potatoes and bacon!

[JACQUES *and* ROBERTA, *famished, dive into the potatoes.*]

GRANDMOTHER-JACQUES: Eat them up! Eat them up!

MOTHER-JACQUES: Eat them up!

JACQUES: [*suddenly the victim of an old qualm, timidly interrupts his
gesture towards the potatoes*] No ... I ...

JACQUELINE: [*to* JACQUES] Aren't you hungry any more?

MOTHER-ROBERT: [*to* JACQUES] You need to eat something!

ROBERTA: [*to* JACQUES] Pusssssy ... yes, eat something ... pussss!
like me!

JACQUES: I'm hungry.

[*He dives into the food.*]

ROBERTA: A bit more potato.

FATHER-JACQUES: [*to* MOTHER-JACQUES] She's got an appetite like
a horse.

[GRANDMOTHER-JACQUES *gives some potatoes and bacon to*
ROBERTA.]

JACQUES: [*to* GRANDMOTHER-JACQUES] Give him some, bacon is
good for the stock.

[GRANDMOTHER-JACQUES *gives* JACQUES *some bacon.*

ROBERTA: A bit more bacon.

[*She is given some.*]

JACQUES: A bit more potato.

[*He is given some.*]

FATHER-JACQUES: That's enough.

MOTHER-JACQUES: Oh! ...

FATHER-JACQUES: I said, enough!

[GRANDMOTHER-JACQUES *takes the dish and sets it down some-where.*]

FATHER-ROBERT: [*to his wife*] That's through meanness rather than principles!

MOTHER-ROBERT: [*to her husband*] Perhaps it's through principles as well!

JACQUELINE: [*to* JACQUES *and* ROBERTA] Make up your minds ... From now on production must be your constant thought.

FATHER-JACQUES: I see that I've got to bring all my authority to bear on this.

MOTHER-JACQUES: You do, my dear, if you feel you want to, of course ... but with care and kindness, please!

MOTHER-ROBERT: We've got the right to bring some of our authority to bear on it, too.

FATHER-ROBERT: If it doesn't work, it's not our daughter's fault, it's certainly not our daughter's fault. Just because she's our only daughter, it doesn't mean she's sterile.

MOTHER-ROBERT: [*to her husband*] That's right. Don't let yourself be put upon.

FATHER-ROBERT: I would like to say ...

FATHER-JACQUES: We must each impose our authority where it is called for.

FATHER-ROBERT: I agree.

FATHER-JACQUES: [*to his son*] Jacques ... I have something very serious to say to you.

[*They form two groups.* JACQUES'S *parents,* GRANDMOTHER-JACQUES *and* JACQUELINE *surround* JACQUES; ROBERTA'S *parents stay with* ROBERTA *withdrawing her slightly from the others.* FATHER-ROBERT *and* MOTHER-ROBERT *speak to their daughter;* ROBERTA *is heard to say docilely from time to time:* 'Yes, papa, yes mamma, yes papa, yes mamma, yes papa, yes mamma.']

FATHER-JACQUES: [*to his son*] Jacques! I have some cruel news for you.

MOTHER-JACQUES: [*weeping*] Beuh! Beuh! Beuh!

JACQUES: What is it, father?

126   IONESCO

FATHER-JACQUES: Look . . . you see your grandmother there. [JACQUELINE *puts a black veil on the* GRANDMOTHER'S *head.*] Don't you notice anything?

JACQUES: No, papa. I don't notice anything.

JACQUELINE: Look harder. Make an effort.

JACQUES: I don't see anything at all.

MOTHER-JACQUES: My son . . . you don't understand! [*To her husband:*] He's at the carefree time of life! [*She weeps on her son's shoulder.*]

GRANDMOTHER-JACQUES: I'm in deep mourning . . .

JACQUES: What does that mean?

[*From her side of the stage, between her parents,* ROBERTA *repeats from time to time:*]

ROBERTA: Yes, papa, yes, mamma . . .

FATHER-JACQUES: A son like you—who for some time now has been a comfort to me, making up his youthful flollies, ought to understand . . .

JACQUELINE: Do you understand?

JACQUES: Understand what, papa, mamma?

FATHER-JACQUES: Well, in a word, this is the awful truth . . . Haven't you ever asked yourself why you don't hear your grandfather singing any longer? . . .

MOTHER-JACQUES: Grandfather who loved you so much and who you adored?

JACQUELINE: [*pointing to the frame*] Or why he is up there? Instead of being here, in our midst?

[*From where he stands,* GRANDFATHER-JACQUES *makes a friendly movement with his head, and smiles.*]

JACQUES: No, I haven't asked myself that.

[*From her side of the stage,* ROBERTA *approves, and continues to say from time to time:*]

ROBERTA: Yes, papa, yes, mamma!

FATHER-JACQUES: If you've never asked yourself about it, now's the time to do so: ask yourself.

JACQUES: I'm asking myself.

JACQUELINE: And what do you answer yourself?

JACQUES: I don't answer anything.

FATHER-JACQUES: [*to his son*] You're not asking yourself hard enough. Ask me.

JACQUES: Ask what?

FATHER-JACQUES: Why don't you hear your grandfather singing any more?

JACQUES: Why don't I hear my grandfather singing any more? Why?

FATHER-JACQUES: I leave it to your grandmother to tell you.

GRANDMOTHER-JACQUES: Because your grandfather is dead.

[JACQUES *makes no reaction of any sort.*]

JACQUELINE: [*to* JACQUES] Grandfather is dead.

[*She gives* JACQUES *a violent nudge.*]

FATHER-JACQUES: Your grandfather is dead.

[*She gives him another nudge.* JACQUES *still makes no reaction. From the* ROBERTS' *corner comes:*]

FATHER-ROBERT: His grandfather is dead.

MOTHER-ROBERT: His grandfather is dead.

ROBERTA: Yes, papa, yes, mamma.

FATHER-JACQUES: [*to his son*] Don't you understand that your grandfather is dead?

JACQUES: No. I don't understand that grandfather is dead.

MOTHER-JACQUES: [*whining*] Poor child. Your reflexes must have stopped working. We must get them going again.

[JACQUES *falls into* JACQUELINE'S *arms, who stands him up again. For a few moments his face remains expressionless. The parents, the grandmother and the sister search for a sign on their son's face. They appear to be very worried.* MOTHER-JACQUES *says:*]

MOTHER-JACQUES: [*to her son*] Cry! Let yourself go, my boy, and cry! [*Silence*] Cry! Come on then! [*Silence. Suddenly* JACQUES *starts to sob.*]

FATHER-JACQUES: There we are, at last! That's done it!

MOTHER JACQUES and

GRANDMOTHER-JACQUES: That's done it! That's done it!

JACQUELINE: That's done it!

JACQUES: Oooh! Oooh! Poor grandfather!

[*He stops and smiles.*]

MOTHER-JACQUES: Again!

JACQUES: [*starting again*] Oooh! Oooh! Poor grandpa!

[ROBERTA *in the* ROBERTS' *corner still repeats but at longer intervals:* 'Yes, papa, yes, mamma.']

MOTHER-JACQUES: [*embracing her weeping son*] My poor baby . . . How he's suffering! . . .

JACQUES: [*weeping*] Hiii! Hiii! Hiii! Hiii! Hiii!

GRANDMOTHER-JACQUES: Yes, it's true, poor grandpa's passed away.

[*She sobs.*]

FATHER-JACQUES: We must all console each other!

[*All the* JACQUES *weep. The* FATHER, *with dignity, wipes away his tears. From the* ROBERTS' *side is heard:*]

MOTHER-ROBERT: Go and offer your cordolences.

FATHER-ROBERT: We must all go; we're part of the family now.

ROBERTA: Yes, papa, yes, mamma.

[ROBERTA, *having moved across to the* JACQUES, *cries:*]

ROBERTA: Heartiest cordolences!

ALL THE JACQUES: [*in chorus, with the exception of* GRANDFATHER-JACQUES] Delighted.

[FATHER-ROBERT, MOTHER-ROBERT, *to* ROBERTA *who turns towards them.*]

MOTHER-ROBERT and

FATHER-ROBERT: Heartiest cordolences!

ROBERTA: Thank you very much. I'm so glad.

[*The three* ROBERTS *now turn to* FATHER-JACQUES.]

THE THREE ROBERTS: [*to* FATHER-JACQUES] Heartiest cordolences!

FATHER-JACQUES: Thank you, my dear friends, I accept them with joy.

THE THREE ROBERTS and

FATHER-JACQUES: [*turning to* MOTHER-JACQUES *and saying, in chorus*] We offer our heartiest cordolences, cordolences, cordolences, cordolences!!

MOTHER-JACQUES: Thank you, thank you, I'm so glad, thank you.

THE THREE ROBERTS:⎫ [*to* GRANDMOTHER-JACQUES] Cordolences,
FATHER-JACQUES: ⎬ cordolences, cordolences, heartiest cor-
MOTHER-JACQUES: ⎭ dolences!

GRANDMOTHER-JACQUES: Thank you so much! Thank you!
  Thank you! I shan't forget, thank you! So nice of you, thank
  you!

THE THREE ROBERTS and

THE THREE JACQUES: [*to* JACQUELINE] Heartiest cordolences!
  Cordolences! Cordolences!

JACQUELINE: Thank you! Thank you! Thank you! Thank you!
  And you, too!
  [*Then, all—with the exception of* GRANDFATHER-JACQUES—
  surround JACQUES *who is the most moved of them all:* 'Cor-
  dolences! Heartiest cordolences! Cordolences! Heartiest cor-
  dolences!']

JACQUES: [*weeping*] Hiiii! Hiiii! Hiiii! Thank you!
  [*Then, when* FATHER-JACQUES *has said:* 'We mustn't forget the
  departed':]

MOTHER-JACQUES: ⎫
FATHER-JACQUES: ⎪
GRANDMOTHER-JACQUES: ⎪ [*in tone in chorus, turned towards the
JACQUES: ⎬ portrait of* GRANDFATHER-JACQUES,
JACQUELINE: ⎪ *with their backs to the audience:*] Cordo-
MOTHER-ROBERT: ⎪ lences! Cordolences! Our heartiest,
FATHER-ROBERT: ⎪ sincerest cordolences! Cordolences!
ROBERTA: ⎭ Cordolences! Cordolences!

  [*One must be able to discern the voice of* JACQUES, *weeping.*]

GRANDFATHER-JACQUES: [*without leaving his frame, replies, with a
  wave of his hand*] Cordolences! Cordolences! Cordolences!
  [*Then all, including* GRANDFATHER-JACQUES *towards whom
  they are turned:* 'Cordolences! Cordolences! Cordolences!
  Cordolences! Heartiest cordolences! Cordolences!' GRAND-
  FATHER-JACQUES *becomes once more motionless in his frame. All
  the characters—with the exception of* GRANDFATHER-JACQUES,
  of course—turn to JACQUES, *surrounding him and saying:*
  'Cordolences! Cordolences! Cordolences! Heartiest cordolences!'*]

Once or twice JACQUES *replies: 'Cordolences!' then resumes his*
weeping with renewed energy. He collapses, as they continue to
offer their cordolences. He is raised up, and installed in a chair.]

JACQUES: [*roaring*] Hiii! Hiiii! Hiiii! Hiiii! Cor-dol-en-ces!
Hiiii!

FATHER-JACQUES: [*stopping his ears, and shouting to* MOTHER-
JACQUES, *even louder than* JACQUES] You've made his reflexes
too sensitive. Desensitize them!

JACQUELINE: [*shouting to* JACQUES] Shut up, you're upsetting
everybody!

MOTHER-ROBERT: [*shouting*] He's gone too far.

[MOTHER-JACQUES *gives* JACQUES *a powerful slap.* JACQUES
stops weeping abruptly. There is a general movement towards
MOTHER-JACQUES, *except for* FATHER-JACQUES. JACQUELINE,
MOTHER-ROBERT, FATHER-ROBERT, ROBERTA, *in tone all*
together:]

TOG. {
THE ROBERT COUPLE: Oh, congratulations, Madame,
warmest congratulations.

GRANDMOTHER-JACQUES

and JACQUELINE: Bravo, Jacques dear! Bravo! Bravo,
mamma! Bravo!

FATHER-JACQUES: That's enough!
[*They all stop instantly. Silence. Everyone looks at* JACQUES.]

FATHER-JACQUES: [*to* JACQUES] It's your right, and your duty, to
know in what circumstances your grandfather met his death!
[GRANDFATHER-JACQUES *in his frame makes a sign.*]

JACQUELINE: Grandfather wants to say something! [GRAND-
FATHER-JACQUES *leaves his frame and comes towards the others.*] He
speaks much better since he died.

FATHER-JACQUES: [*to* JACQUES] Here comes your grandfather, fit
as a fiddle, to tell you himself how he met his death.
[*Respectful silence. As* GRANDFATHER-JACQUES *approaches, the*
others hold their noses.]

GRANDFATHER-JACQUES: [*very proud of being the centre of attention*]
Hmmm! Hmmm! It all passed off very well, passed away . . .
I was in the middle of a song . . . [*He is about to sing.*]

GRANDMOTHER-JACQUES: You're not going to start singing again . . . You're dead. You're in mourning.

GRANDFATHER-JACQUES: No . . . No . . . No . . . That doesn't matter. I feel like singing.

FATHER-JACQUES [*to* GRANDFATHER-JACQUES] If you show no respect for your own grief, how do you expect others to? . . . Carry on with the story, only faster!

GRANDFATHER-JACQUES: I'll sing it!

GRANDMOTHER-JACQUES: You're not going to sing.

GRANDFATHER-JACQUES: Then I shan't say a word. Not another word. That's the last you'll see of me. There!

[GRANDFATHER-JACQUES *goes back to his frame.*]

GRANDMOTHER-JACQUES: Still as obstinate as ever! It hasn't taught him anything!

[*In his frame,* GRANDFATHER-JACQUES *looks sullen and moody in contrast to his air of gaiety at the beginning of the play. He will not move again until the end.*]

FATHER-JACQUES: [*to his son*] You see how it is, my boy, we all have to go! You're our one and only hope! It's essential, absolutely essential, that we replace those that pass away. Grandfather is dead, long live grandfather.

ALL TOGETHER: [*except for* JACQUES, *who is nonplussed*] Grandfather is dead, long live grandfather.

JACQUES: Why?

FATHER-JACQUES: We must assure the continuity of our race.

JACQUES: Why?

FATHER-JACQUES: The continuity of our race . . . the white race! Long live the white race!

[*All, except* JACQUES, *applaud and say together:* 'Long live the white race! Long live the white race!']

FATHER-JACQUES: [*to his son*] The future of the white race is in your hands. It must go on, go on and extend its power more and more!

JACQUES: What can we do?

JACQUELINE: If it's to go on, we must stop it from going back.

JACQUES: Through what means?

FATHER-JACQUES: [*to his son*] Through production. Whatever disappears must be replaced by new products, more numerous and varied than before. It's up to you to instigate production . . .

MOTHER-JACQUES: [*to her son*] My son, if you want me to be proud of you, try and instigate, instigate production . . .

[ROBERTA *looks embarrassed.*]

FATHER-ROBERT: My daughter is perfectly capable of it—as I've already officially declared.

[ROBERTA *looks more and more embarrassed.*]

FATHER-JACQUES: We shall soon see whether these last three years are going to yield good results. Up to now they don't seem to me to have been very remarkable!

[ROBERTA, *more and more embarrassed, assumes nevertheless extravagant poses.*]

MOTHER-ROBERT: [*to* ROBERTA] Now come on, dear, that's not very nice in front of everyone. Come with mamma, I'll teach you. All you need is a bit of training.

MOTHER-JACQUES: [*to* MOTHER-ROBERT] If my experience can be of any help to you. . . . Don't hesitate to ask.

MOTHER-ROBERT: With pleasure. We'd be only too happy.

GRANDMOTHER-JACQUES: [*to* MOTHER-ROBERT] I'll come as well. I'll sing her a lullaby . . .

MOTHER-ROBERT: [*to* FATHER-ROBERT] You stay here with your son-in-law. If we need you for the element, we'll call you. [*To* FATHER-JACQUES:] We'll call you, too, if we find we need some element.

FATHER-JACQUES: [*bowing*] I'm here whenever you need me.

MOTHER-JACQUES: I've got some element, I've got some in reserve, if it's needed.

[ROBERTA, MOTHER-ROBERT, MOTHER-JACQUES *and* GRAND-MOTHER-JACQUES *leave right.*] ROBERTA *exits making gestures and assuming more and more extravagant attitudes. As he sees her leaving,* JACQUES *makes a vague gesture with his arms towards her, pulls a grimace like a child who wants to cry, saying: 'Mm . . . Mm . . . Mm . . .'*]

JACQUELINE: [*watching* ROBERTA *and the others leaving*] She already looks quite maternal. She's got an instinct for it.

[JACQUES *flops into a chair*.]

FATHER-ROBERT: [*to* JACQUES] We'll soon see what you're made of.

FATHER-JACQUES: [*to* JACQUES] Jacques, my son, pluck up your courage. Produce something! Be a man!

JACQUELINE: Come on, come on, where's your courage!

FATHER-ROBERT: Come on, come on, where's your courage! Get going!

JACQUELINE: Get going. Start pushing.

[JACQUES *grimaces. He settles in his chair*.]

JACQUELINE: Go on . . . Go on . . .

FATHER-ROBERT: Go on, go on, be a man. We've all had to go through it.

FATHER-JACQUES: [*in a powerful voice, to his son*] Hurry up, or you'll have me to deal with.

VOICE OF MOTHER-JACQUES: Is it working over there?

JACQUELINE: [*to* JACQUES] Get on with it, they're getting impatient. Push.

FATHER-ROBERT: [*to* JACQUES] Push.

JACQUES: [*grimacing*] It doesn't happen just like that . . . you can't do it to order . . . I don't feel any inspiration.

VOICE OF MOTHER-JACQUES: Jacques, Roberta is ready. Are you?

VOICE OF MOTHER-ROBERT: You won't be able to say it's my daughter's fault any more.

FATHER-JACQUES: Jacques, don't be so lazy.

JACQUELINE: [*shouting so as to be heard on the other side*] Just a minute, be patient for a moment . . .

JACQUES: [*in his chair*] It's coming . . . I feel it's going to come . . .

VOICE OF GRANDMOTHER-JACQUES: Jacques, my baby, get a move on, do . . . Roberta's been ready for some time. She can't go on waiting.

JACQUES: I'm doing what I can.

FATHER-JACQUES: That's not amounting to much.

FATHER-ROBERT: [*to* JACQUES] Come on, show some grit.

JACQUELINE: Show some grit . . .

FATHER-ROBERT [*to* FATHER-JACQUES] Your son, it seems to me, is not worthy of my daughter.

FATHER-JACQUES: It seems to me, the die is not yet cast. We'll see about that later.

JACQUELINE: [*to the portrait of* GRANDFATHER-JACQUES] Do something, grandfather.

GRANDFATHER-JACQUES: [*sardonic, motionless*] Ah ... ah ... ah ... I couldn't care less ... I'm not in this world any longer ... what's more, you wouldn't let me sing ... that'll teach you ... serves you right ...

JACQUELINE: [*to* GRANDFATHER-JACQUES] Then keep your mouth shut.

GRANDFATHER-JACQUES: [*very fast; furious*] I'll keep my mouth shut if I feel like it, and if I don't, I won't, who do you think you are, what about the cult of the dead?

FATHER-ROBERT: [*to* GRANDFATHER-JACQUES] You shut up, Sir.

FATHER-JACQUES: [*threateningly*] Shut up!

[GRANDFATHER-JACQUES *does so.*]

VOICE OF MOTHER-ROBERT: Well, how's it going?

JACQUES: [*clutching his stomach*] Aie! Aie! Aie! Aie!

GRANDFATHER-JACQUES: [*laughing in his frame*] Hee! Hee! Hee!

FATHER-ROBERT: [*to* GRANDFATHER-JACQUES] Do I have to call for order?!

JACQUES: [*hands on his stomach*] Aie! Aie! Aie! Aie! Aie! Aie!

[*His cries get more and more shrill.*]

JACQUELINE: [*calling to the others*] Mamma, mamma, it's happening, he's having his labour pains!

FATHER-ROBERT: [*shouting*] Roberta ... Roberta ... you can let go now!

[*He goes out right.*]

JACQUES: [*in agony*] Aie! Aie! Aie! Aie!

VOICE OF MOTHER-ROBERT: Let go, my dear! ... You can let go now ...

VOICE OF ROBERTA: [*very shrill*] Co-co-codac! Co-co-codac! Co-co-codac! Co-co-codac! Co-co-codac! Co-co-codac! Co-co-codac! Co-co-codac! Co-co-codac!

JACQUES: Aie! Aie! Aie! Aie!

[MOTHER-ROBERT, MOTHER-JACQUES, GRANDMOTHER-JACQUES *appear right*.]

VOICE OF ROBERTA: Co-co-co-co-co-codac!

[*The loud 'co-co-codacs!' of* ROBERTE *continue to be heard.* JACQUES *groans.* MOTHER-ROBERT *and* MOTHER-JACQUES *fall into each other's arms.*]

MOTHER-ROBERT: Jacques's dear little mother ... our children! [*Tears*]

MOTHER-JACQUES: Roberta's dear little mother ... our own little ones! [*In tears.*]

[*The 'co-co-codacs' get even louder.* JACQUES *makes a groaning 'Ah', and faints.*]

TOG. { MOTHER-JACQUES: Ah! My son! My son!
{ GRANDMOTHER-JACQUES: Now, now! It's no time for that!

FATHER-JACQUES: Jacqueline! Your brother's fainted!

[*All the characters rush to surround* JACQUES, *rubbing his temples, administering little slaps, during which time one hears:*]

VOICE OF FATHER-ROBERT: That's it now! Bring a basket!

FATHER-JACQUES: It's been too much for him! It's too much for him!

[*General feverish movement. Agitated fluttering round* JACQUES, *and also towards off-stage right whence the 'co-dacs' come.* JACQUELINE *goes out right, carrying an empty basket, as* JACQUES *recovers consciousness.*]

MOTHER-JAQUES: My boy! He's coming to!

JACQUES: Where am I?

MOTHER-JACQUES: At home, my dear, with your own loving parents!

MOTHER-ROBERT: In your darling Roberta's own castle!

JACQUES: [*disgusted*] Oh, I want to get away!

FATHER-ROBERT: [*appears right, carrying the basket full of eggs*] Here are the first eggs!

ALL: [*except* JACQUES, *who is slumped in a chair, whilst* GRAND-FATHER-JACQUES *watches him out of one eye*] Aaah! Aaah! Bravo!

[*They applaud, embrace and congratulate each other.*]

FATHER-JACQUES and

FATHER-ROBERT: [*congratulating each other*] Congratulations!
Congratulations!

> [*The two* MOTHERS *embrace, weeping, whilst* GRANDMOTHER-
> JACQUES, *having seized the basket of eggs, exclaims:* 'Oh, aren't
> they pretty! They're so sweet! What a size! I do hope they're
> not addled!' *The various characters now move and encircle*
> GRANDMOTHER-JACQUES; *they take the basket. This scene takes
> place down-stage.*]

FATHER-JACQUES: They're beautifully fresh, they must be worth
twenty francs a piece. We could have them boiled.

MOTHER-ROBERT: They're my daughter's very first eggs! They
look just like her!

GRANDMOTHER-JACQUES: Oh no, they're the spitting image of
Jacques.

FATHER-ROBERT: I don't agree.

MOTHER-JACQUES: They haven't got three noses!

MOTHER-ROBERT: That's because they're too small. They'll
grow later.

MOTHER-JACQUES: Nonsense, they look like both of them.

FATHER-JACQUES: Where is Jacqueline?

FATHER-ROBERT: She's with Roberta. Someone has to be there
to help her.

MOTHER-JACQUES: I feel quite moved! It's a wonderful moment!

FATHER-JACQUES: [*takes the basket, moves towards his son, with the
others*] Look, these are your own eggs!

JACQUES: Thank you.

FATHER-JACQUES: Now you must hatch them out.

MOTHER-JACQUES: He may be too tired at the moment.

FATHER-ROBERT: Our daughter can do her own hatching!

FATHER-JACQUES: In our family it's the man's job! [*To* JACQUES:]
Come on, get up!

> [*They all raise* JACQUES *up, who is exhausted, and bear him to
> the hatching table.*]

FATHER-JACQUES: [*carrying his son*] Carry him on to the hatching
table!

MOTHER-ROBERT: [*carrying* JACQUES, *to her husband*] You always let people get the better of you. You're not very smart.

GRANDMOTHER-JACQUES: [*carrying* JACQUES] You're married, I'm very happy about that. Now you've got to hatch!
[*They heave* JACQUES *on to the table.*]

MOTHER-JACQUES: Hatch well, my boy!

GRANDMOTHER-JACQUES: Like your forefathers did!

GRANDFATHER-JACQUES: [*in his frame*] Hee! Hee! Hee! [*It is a sardonic laugh.*]

FATHER-JACQUES: Hatch, hatch in the name of glory and for the greatness of nations, and for immortality.
[*The 'Co-co-codacs', which have stopped, now start up again with even greater force.*]

FATHER-ROBERT: We must hurry! The eggs will start piling up!
[JACQUES *is installed on, or in the middle of, his eggs.* JACQUELINE *appears, carrying a second basket of eggs.*]

ALL: [*except for* JACQUES, *and* GRANDFATHER-JACQUES *who laughs silently*] Bravo! Bravo! Oh, they're lovely!

FATHER-ROBERT: I'm going to get the others!
[*He goes out right.*]

JACQUELINE: There's still a lot more!

FATHER-JACQUES: [*lifts up* JACQUES *who is lying flat on his stomach, takes a look, and says*] You can bring some more! There's still room! Don't worry!
[*He empties the contents of the basket on and around* JACQUES.]

MOTHER-ROBERT: Bring them! Bring them here!

FATHER-JACQUES: Come on, come on, don't stop!

JACQUES: I'm hot . . .

MOTHER-JACQUES: [*to* JACQUES] That's what you need, my dear, to hatch . . . warmth, and a lot of love! . . .
[*She sponges her son's brow.*]

FATHER-JACQUES: [*clapping his hands*] Production! Production! Production!

GRANDMOTHER-JACQUES: Eggs! Eggs! Eggs! Eggs!
[*She leaps and dances.*]

MOTHER-JACQUES: Hatch, hatch, my son, hatch!

[JACQUELINE *takes out the empty basket as* FATHER-ROBERT *comes in with a third full one. The 'Co-co-codacs' continue* .]

ALL: Bravo! Bravo!

FATHER-ROBERT: There's more still!

JACQUES: [*puffing noisily like a steam engine*] Tuff! Tuff! Tuff! Tuff! Tuff! Tuff!

[*The rhythm of his 'Tuff Tuffs' steadily accelerates and so do the 'Co-co-codacs', as well as the movements of* FATHER-ROBERT *and* JACQUELINE *as they dart ceaselessly to and fro, fetching and carrying the egg baskets; the action is so arranged that as one of them arrives the other leaves, and vice-versa.*]

FATHER-JACQUES: Long live production! Still more production! Produce! Produce!

JACQUES: Tuff! Tuff! Tuff! Tuff!

['*Co-co-codacs' from the side.*]

MOTHER-JACQUES: [*sponging his brow*] Bear up ... bear up ...

JACQUES: I'm very hot, mamma. Tuff! Tuff!

MOTHER-ROBERT: Keep going, don't stop!

FATHER-JACQUES: [*tapping his hands together*] Production! Production! Production! [*etc.*]

[*The general movement increases.* MOTHER-ROBERT *takes the egg baskets alternately from* FATHER-ROBERT *and* JACQUELINE, *and pours the contents on* JACQUES' *head and body, on the table and on the ground.* JACQUES *becomes quite covered in them; and* MOTHER-ROBERT, *handing back the empty baskets, says:*]

MOTHER-ROBERT: Production! Production! Production! [*etc.*]

[GRANDMOTHER-JACQUES, *in the centre of the stage, also claps her hands as she spins round, saying: 'Production! Production! Production!' etc. The movement and the noise continue: 'Co-co-codac!' 'Tuff! Tuff! Tuff!' 'Production! Production!' become a chorused refrain whilst, without interrupting the action and the comings and goings, one hears, in voices loud enough to surmount the tumult, the following speeches:*]

MOTHER-JACQUES: I keep thinking of the future of all these children!

MOTHER-ROBERT: What are we going to make of the offspring?

FATHER-JACQUES: Sausage meat!

FATHER-ROBERT: [*between his comings and goings*] Cannon fodder!

GRANDMOTHER-JACQUES: We'll need some for omelettes.

JACQUELINE: [*between her comings and goings*] Some can be athletes!

MOTHER-JACQUES: We'll keep some back for reproduction.

MOTHER-ROBERT: And for modelling paste.

FATHER-ROBERT: And pastry paste.

FATHER-JACQUES: We'll make officers, officials, and officious people.

GRANDMOTHER-JACQUES: And we'll put some aside to eat ourselves.

JACQUELINE: Valets and masters!

FATHER-JACQUES: Diplomats.

MOTHER-JACQUES: Knitting wool.

[*In his frame,* GRANDFATHER-JACQUES *can direct the action, with a finger, like an orchestra leader.*]

MOTHER-ROBERT: Leeks and onions.

FATHER-ROBERT: Bankers and pigs.

FATHER-JACQUES: Citizens and country yokels.

MOTHER-JACQUES: Employers and employees!

JACQUELINE: Popes, kings and emperors.

FATHER-JACQUES: Policemen.

MOTHER-ROBERT: Solicitors and parsons.

GRANDMOTHER-JACQUES: Omelettes! Lots of omelettes!

JACQUELINE: Humanitarians and anti-humanitarians!

[*After this last remark, the refrain becomes:* 'Yes, yes, yes!'; *with only* FATHER-JACQUES *continuing with his former refrain of* 'Production! Production! Production!' *and still clapping his hands.*]

MOTHER-JACQUES: Opportunists!

MOTHER-ROBERT: Nationalists!

FATHER-ROBERT: Internationalists!

FATHER-JACQUES: Revolutionaries!

GRANDMOTHER-JACQUES: Anti-revolutionaries!

JACQUELINE: Radishes! Radicals!

MOTHER-JACQUES: Proletarians!

FATHER-ROBERT: Householders!

FATHER-JACQUES: Housebreakers!

GRANDMOTHER-JACQUES: Chemists.

JACQUELINE: Firemen, teachers.

MOTHER-JACQUES: Jansenists.

MOTHER-ROBERT: Free thinkers.

FATHER-ROBERT: Marxists. Marquis, marks and counter-marks.

FATHER-JACQUES: Idealists. Relativists.

GRANDMOTHER-JACQUES: Existentialists.

JACQUELINE: Essentialists and materialists.

MOTHER-JACQUES: Federalists and spiritualists.

MOTHER-ROBERT: Intellectuals.

FATHER-ROBERT: Brothers, half-brothers!

FATHER-JACQUES: Friends and enemies!

GRANDMOTHER-JACQUES: Army cooks!

JACQUELINE: Customs officials, actors!

MOTHER-JACQUES: Drunkards and Catholics.

MOTHER-ROBERT: Protestants and Israelites!

FATHER-ROBERT: Stairs and shoes.

FATHER-JACQUES: Pencils and pen-holders.

MOTHER-ROBERT: Aspirins! Matches!

GRANDMOTHER-JACQUES: And omelettes! Above all, lots of omelettes!

[JACQUELINE *and* FATHER-ROBERT *are standing centre stage, empty baskets in their hands.*]

ALL TOGETHER IN CHORUS: [*except for* JACQUES *and* GRANDFATHER-JACQUES] Yes, yes, omelettes, lots of omelettes.

[*The movement and noise cease abruptly.* JACQUES *is heard to say in a feeble voice:*]

JACQUES: And pessimists!

ALL: [*indignant*] What? How dare he? What's the matter with him? Is he still going on? Never content!

[*They move towards him. Tense silence.*]

JACQUES: Anarchists. And nihilists.

FATHER-ROBERT: I said, we could never rely on him.

FATHER-JACQUES: [*to his son*] Have you lost your faith?

MOTHER-ROBERT: He hasn't got any faith.

FATHER-JACQUES: [*to his son*] Then say what it is you want!

JACQUES: I want a fountain of light, incandescent water, fire of ice, snows of fire.

JACQUELINE: [*to* JACQUES] Don't forget your obligations.

GRANDFATHER-JACQUES: [*in his frame, to* JACQUES] Look after your eggs!

FATHER-ROBERT: [*to* JACQUES] You can always go to the firework displays.

MOTHER-ROBERT: He's certainly got some big ideas!

FATHER-ROBERT: Why not go to the Chateau of Merdailles?

ALL: Long live production! Long live the white race! Keep it up! Keep it up!

> [*The cries of 'Production!' and 'Co-co-codac' start up again, the action speeds up even more in the general enthusiasm.* GRAND-FATHER-JACQUES *in his frame also cries out: 'Produce! Produce!!' The others say 'Let's produce! Let's produce!'; they all give out 'Co-co-codacs', and applaud.*]

GRANDFATHER-JACQUES: As it was in the past, the future lies in eggs!

> [*A trap-door may or may not open; or perhaps the stage may or may not slowly collapse, and the characters—all unwittingly— gently sink and disappear without interrupting their actions—or just quite simply carry on, according to the technical facilities available.*]

CURTAIN